RAISING
YOUR
Grandchildren

Titles in the
GRANDPARENTING MATTERS
Series

Equipping Grandparents

Biblical Grandparenting

Grandparenting

Grandparenting DVD

Long-Distance Grandparenting

Overcoming Grandparenting Barriers

Discipling Your Grandchildren

Raising Your Grandchildren

"For all the grandparents who find themselves back on the front lines, raising your grandchildren, keep this book by your side. It is packed with essential Scriptures and stories to encourage and guide you through the journey ahead."

—Dr. Rob Rienow, founder of Visionary Family Ministries

"In *Raising Your Grandchildren*, Cavin Harper offers a much-needed theological perspective into parenting as a grandparent, offering hope to those who are suddenly thrust into the unexpected role of rearing their children's children. Recognizing the hardships of older adults caring full-time for the young, he also shows how the eternal benefits for both grandparents and grandchildren far outweigh the temporary difficulties. I highly recommend this honest, hopeful, and insightful guide."

—Denise George, co-author of *Called to Forgive*

"As a friend and grandparent who has known and watched Cavin Harper's passion for equipping grandparents over the past twenty years, I enthusiastically recommend his book, *Raising Your Grandchildren*, as a biblical and practical guide for leaving a legacy to the next generation."

—Larry C. Griffith, former director of development for Ravi Zacharias Ministries

"If you are a grandparent raising your grandchildren, Cavin's words are full of practical guidance, but more than that, they provide grace-filled hope that our Good Shepherd is with you every step of the way. If you are a ministry leader, I pray this book opens your eyes and hearts to these families who are sitting in your pews."

—Pastor Matt Ferrell, Rockrimmon campus pastor, Woodmen Valley Chapel

"Cavin's book gives voice and encouragement to a growing group of underserved and misunderstood grandparents who are unexpectedly parenting for the second time around. It is compassionate and truth-filled. In a confusing and often heartbreaking world, Cavin reminds us to go to the only true source of hope—God's Word."

—Kristin Orphan, MS, founder and
executive director of Finally Home

"Cavin Harper is truly the father of the grandparenting movement in this country. *Raising Your Grandchildren* is outstanding! It is a no-nonsense read that gets straight to the point. I think this book would help any grandparent raising their own grandchildren."

—Jere Vincent, president of Family Builders Ministries

RAISING
YOUR
Grandchildren

Encouragement and Guidance for Those Parenting Their Children's Children

CAVIN HARPER

DR. JOSH MULVIHILL, GENERAL EDITOR

BETHANYHOUSE

a division of Baker Publishing Group
Minneapolis, Minnesota

© 2020 by Legacy Coalition, Cavin Harper, and Josh Mulvihill

Published by Bethany House Publishers
11400 Hampshire Avenue South
Bloomington, Minnesota 55438
www.bethanyhouse.com

Bethany House Publishers is a division of
Baker Publishing Group, Grand Rapids, Michigan

Printed in the United States of America

Library of Congress Cataloging-in-Publication Data
Names: Harper, Cavin, author. | Mulvihill, Josh, editor.
Title: Raising your grandchildren : encouragement and guidance for those parenting their children's children / Cavin Harper ; General editor Josh Mulvihill.
Description: Minneapolis, Minnesota : Bethany House Publishers, [2021] | Series: Grandparenting matters
Identifiers: LCCN 2020011367 | ISBN 9780764231339 (paper) | ISBN 9781493429776 (ebook)
Subjects: LCSH: Grandparents as parents—United States. | Grandparent and child—United States. | Grandchildren—United States.
Classification: LCC HQ759.9 .H3647 2021 | DDC 649/.10853—dc23
LC record available at https://lccn.loc.gov/2020011367

All dates, place names, titles, and events in this account are factual. The names of certain individuals have been changed in order to protect their privacy.

Cover design by Dan Pitts.

Josh Mulvihill and Legacy Coalition are represented by William Denzel.

20 21 22 23 24 25 26   7 6 5 4 3 2 1

CONTENTS

Series Preface   9

Introduction   13

A Word from Rachel Mahnke   17

1. We Didn't Sign Up for This   19

2. The Guilt-Blame Trap   25

3. When Faith Is Put to the Test   33

4. You Keep Using That Word   45

5. You Can't Give What You Do Not Have   53

6. Shepherd-Driven Soul Care   63

7. More Than Good Grandparents   73

8. The One Another Factor   87

9. A Plea to Pastors and Church Leaders   97

Appendix   103

Notes   107

Acknowledgments   109

SERIES PREFACE

GRANDPARENTING MATTERS is a series of short books that address common grandparenting problems with biblical solutions and practical ideas. I have had the joy of talking with grandparents all over the country about their God-designed role in the lives of children and grandchildren. Regularly, questions arise about how to do what the Bible says in the midst of barriers, problems, and challenges.

Grandparenting is filled with many joys, but it can also be filled with unexpected pain and problems. Relational tensions, grandparenting restrictions, adult prodigals, grandparents as parents, divorce, long-distance relationships, and blended families all can cause the heart to ache. When brokenness touches our families, we naturally ask questions about how to navigate the challenges.

There are a growing number of resources for Christian grandparents that address the purpose of grandparenting, but few deal with the problem-solving side of family life. We created this series because problems are common, hope is needed, and God's Word provides guidance that can be applied to our unique situations. This series aims simultaneously to comfort and encourage, to equip and edify, and also to point the way ahead. If you are discouraged or hurting, then I trust you will be blessed by this series. If you are looking for biblical solutions and practical how-tos, you will find them in these pages.

We've titled the series GRANDPARENTING MATTERS because we believe the Bible teaches that the grandparent-grandchild relationship is important and worthy of our time and attention. Grandparents have a significant impact on the spiritual lives of grandchildren that is second only to parents. Our prayer is that the gospel is proclaimed, God is honored, your family experiences healing and health, and your children and children's children know, love, and serve Jesus.

Cavin Harper has been a friend and ministry partner for many years. I've had the joy of watching Cavin minister to grandparents nationally as well as faithfully serve his own family. He is a man of strong Christian character and great integrity. He practices what he preaches. He also is the founder and president of the Christian Grandparent Network that he has been leading for over two decades. Until recently, it was the only ministry in North America that was specifically focused on equipping Christian grandparents to reach and disciple their families. Before launching the Christian Grandparent Network, Cavin was a pastor for nearly two decades. Cavin has a lifetime of ministry experience. Cavin doesn't chase the latest ministry fads but is fully committed to the gospel of Christ, the authority of Scripture, and the power of prayer.

No one expects to be a grandparent raising a grandchild. Individuals who find themselves in this unexpected place of life arrive there not because of joyful circumstances but because of painful ones. Cavin has written a very practical book that is full of compassion and will help individuals find hope in Christ and strength for the journey ahead. If you are a grandparent raising a grandchild, you should read this book.

If you are new to the GRANDPARENTING MATTERS series, I want to encourage you to check out some of the other books in the series, such as *Grandparenting, Biblical Grandparenting, Long-Distance Grandparenting,* and *Overcoming Grandparenting Barriers.* I'm delighted by the high caliber of authors in this series and the impact these books will have on families for their good and for the glory of God. I trust you will be blessed by Cavin's godly wisdom, gain a renewed hope in God, experience joy in Christ despite trying circumstances, and become better equipped to be a disciple-making grandparent who passes on a heritage of faith to future generations.

—Dr. Josh Mulvihill

Founding Member, the Legacy Coalition
Executive Director of Church and Family Ministry, Renewanation
Connect with me at GospelShapedFamily.com

INTRODUCTION

When I began a ministry to grandparents in 1997, it never crossed my mind to address grandparents parenting their own grandchildren. I knew there were a fair number of grandparents in that situation, but I had no idea how significant this issue was until I recently began hearing many of your stories.

Your cries for help have not gone unnoticed, and the depth of your pain, physical exhaustion, and astounding circumstances are beginning to be recognized. I have been blessed by the inexpressible joy that I've observed by many grandparents raising grandchildren as you pour yourselves out for these young lives you love so deeply.

I am writing this book to encourage readers who find themselves in this difficult life situation. I'm also compelled to tell your stories because I realize that grandparents raising grandchildren are often ignored and unnoticed.

Grandparents who are raising their grandchildren is a growing demographic. Some studies, mostly from state and federal social service agencies, suggest 2.6 million grandchildren in the United States are being raised by grandparents, but that only

13

accounts for those who enter the foster care system.[1] I believe that number is low. The 2010 Census indicates approximately 8 percent of all grandchildren in the United States are being raised by grandparents. That number increased to 10 percent in 2012, which means that approximately eight to ten million kids in 2012 were being raised by grandparents. That number could be as high as twelve million today. Some grandparents do not have custody of their grandchildren but operate as a second parent by watching the grandchild for numerous days each week or providing significant emotional and financial support to a single-parent home.

Most states report drug and opioid addictions to be the number-one cause of child removals from parental care. Such addictions result in an estimated 40 percent of children who are removed from parental care and placed in the home of a grandparent.[2]

There is a lack of research to identify the critical needs of grandparents in this arena of grandparenting, but thankfully the Supporting Grandparents Raising Grandchildren Act was signed into law in July 2018 to provide further research and recommendations for coordinating the support of grandparents raising their grandchildren, especially due to the opioid epidemic. This growing awareness may help give us a better picture of how large this demographic really is.

Whatever the actual numbers are, I hope you recognize you are not the only one living this story. That doesn't change the challenges you face or the exhaustion you feel, but I hope it encourages you to know that you are not alone. Hopefully churches will recognize this reality and the growing need in this area of family life and see it as a significant ministry opportunity.

I owe a major debt of gratitude to Rachel Mahnke, a grandmother raising two of her grandchildren, for her courage to come forward, seek help, and teach me how significant this matter is today. I am humbled to have the privilege of working alongside Rachel and her husband, Lee, in this journey of understanding and engaging scores of grandparents like yourself.

Rachel's story will be woven throughout this book, along with the stories of others who are in the thick of this new and unexpected responsibility. I know her story will be a blessing to you. While this book may not include your specific story, I am confident one or more stories I've shared will resonate with you.

My prayer is to be a voice of encouragement to you as well as a spokesperson for those who are often invisible in churches and communities. I wrote this book to communicate God's love, grace, and hope to you when you find yourself feeling overwhelmed and wondering if you can get through it. I am aware of the voiceless anguish many of you experience and of your desire to be seen—to know someone wants to help bear your burden.

I say *burden* not because I believe that you view your decision to love and care for your grandchildren as a burden, but because of the weight of unimaginable challenges that accompany sacrificial love. Most grandparents raising grandchildren bear financial burdens, many bear guilt or shame, and almost all experience some measure of relational burden. Too often you bear these alone.

I want you to know you are not alone. My hope is that this book will be a source of hope and a means God uses to provide the strength to endure. For unknown reasons, God has providentially placed precious children in your hands to parent and love, and it is my desire that these pages encourage you to persevere and provide the confidence to make a difference in your grandchildren's lives for eternity.

Though a mystery to me, but not to God, I believe He has called me to bring this message of hope into your story. I believe God wants to give you reason to trust in His lavish grace and mercy, so that you will be strengthened with power through His Spirit for this grand calling that has been entrusted to you for such a time as this.

—Cavin T. Harper

Founder and President,
Christian Grandparenting Network

A WORD FROM RACHEL MAHNKE

Cavin mentioned that you will be reading portions of my story throughout this book. After working as a teacher for many years, I felt that God was showing me it was time to be a student and learn all I could about our new role in life. Yet, how was I to care for these traumatized, fragile babies? With a baby crying for hours every day, how was I going to find joy in my new circumstances? How was I going to maintain my relationship with my husband and with other family members and friends whom I desperately needed in my life?

I read every book I could get my hands on but discovered there was very little that addressed my new role. With two grandbabies under the age of two, you can probably imagine the challenge of finding time to do anything but care for them. But I persisted, in the strength of the Lord.

As you read through this book, you will encounter personal snapshots related to my journey, how I learned to cope with my new reality, what we did to regain connection to a life that was now dramatically changed, and how my husband and I began to thrive, not just survive. Perhaps my story will encourage you in yours.

1

We Didn't Sign Up for This

Darlene knew the call would be coming.

Her youngest daughter was addicted to heroin. Her drug habit had begun when she was introduced to opioids. Eventually, her addiction left her homeless with two children, ages one and two. Darlene made the call to the Department of Human Services for their protection, knowing something had to be done for the sake of those children. The authorities tracked down Darlene's daughter and brought the two children to Darlene and Ted, the nearest relatives. That was five years ago. Nothing much has changed for her daughter, but at least the grandchildren now have a stable home.

Ted and Darlene love their grandchildren and are doing their best to raise them, but it has not been easy. Born into drugs and domestic violence, the children have numerous behavioral issues. As they seek to cope with what it means to parent again, Ted and Darlene feel very isolated, if not abandoned, especially by family members. Despite all this, they are resolute. When I spoke with Darlene, she told me, "Ted and I are committed to seeing this through together."

Among millennials like their daughter, the opioid epidemic is impacting millions of young adults and taking its toll on their families. Sadly, it's not only those who are caught in the grip of drug addiction who pay the price. Their children and the grandparents of those children also become victims.

For these grandparents, life has shifted from the role of cheerleader and coach for their adult children, to assuming the role of parent once again. No grandparent imagines that one day they will need to assume the role of parent to their grandchildren. Not in their wildest dreams would a grandparent expect this to happen to them.

Ted and Darlene's story may not be your story. The opioid epidemic is only one of many reasons grandparents end up becoming parents for their grandchildren. The circumstances that lead to grandparents raising grandchildren are as varied as the people involved. The five most common reasons associated with this tragic event are

1. Drugs (including alcoholism)
2. Domestic violence
3. Detention (jail or prison)
4. Divorce
5. Death

Whatever the unfortunate cause, it ultimately comes down to young parents not being able to protect and provide for their own children.

If one of the first four situations describes your situation, you may be among those who still cling to the hope that your adult child or their spouse will one day be in a position to properly care for and raise your grandchildren. You hope your parenting role will be temporary.

But many individuals have no such expectation. You may have full parental rights as a result of court-awarded adoption rights and are now the legal parents. Or you may have a range of roles, from full guardianship to temporary custody. You might even have no legal status at all, choosing to not involve the courts and social services. Yet the grandchildren are living with you because either the parents asked you to do it or because you took action to intervene for the protection of the child.

Grandparents raising grandchildren is nothing new. It has been going on for much of human history. In some cultures, grandparents are part of an extended family, either living together or in close proximity. They are a functional part of the entire family dynamic and a critical factor in the raising of the children in the family.

In many of our inner-city communities in the United States and Canada, a large number of children are raised by a grandparent (usually a grandmother), even if a biological parent is present (usually not a father). Many individuals do it with very limited resources to help them.

What has changed is the growing number of grandparents across all socioeconomic lines who are caught in the consequences of a growing opioid epidemic. Like Ted and Darlene, these families are forced to face the reality of being parents once again. Only this time the expectation of a joyous arrival is not part of the package. For many, life is suddenly and unexpectedly interrupted by a phone call or knock on the door in the middle of the night. There is no time to anticipate anything—only to react and try to understand the implications of this new way of life.

Yet this "unexpected interruption" is not the end of the story, is it? My goal for this book is to help you recognize the hand of our sovereign God in this "interruption" and seize upon it as an "unexpected opportunity," even though, admittedly, it may be a hard one. I hope to encourage you in this journey to embrace the amazing opportunities you have been given to influence one or more children to know who they are, whose they are, and why they are so precious to you and their heavenly Father.

In the numerous encounters I have had with grandparents in a situation similar to yours, I have observed there are at least seven feelings that, in varying degrees, are common to most grandparents raising grandchildren. I have also observed that those unfamiliar with your reality are largely unaware of these feelings. Even if some of these are not relevant to you, they are still significant for many other grandparents raising grandchildren. See if you resonate with any of these feelings.

- Feeling emotionally and mentally overwhelmed
- Feeling physically exhausted
- Feeling hopeless (which may lead to depression)
- Feeling isolated from others (friends, family, church)
- Feeling guilt and shame (*Was I a failure as a parent, and will I only repeat those failures with my grandchild[ren]?*)
- Feeling judged and/or misunderstood by others (particularly from family members or church people)
- Feeling lost and helpless (*I don't know what to do or where to turn for help*)

My hope is to be an instrument of God in which He will heap a great measure of hope upon you. I believe the Bible is the sufficient source of truth and hope that will help you navigate these feelings. Jesus came to testify to the truth and to remind us that He has already overcome all the troubles that life may dump on us. I believe the gospel of Christ is immensely valuable for your life situation. The gospel is not just some theological mumbo jumbo, but it is real-life practical truths that you can put into practice to strengthen you and lead you into the place of rest found in God's peace.

Before we jump into those practical truths, I want to remind you of something that is easily forgotten. As a grandparent suddenly thrust into this new role of parenting and providing a stable home for your children's children, I want you to know you are not the only parent with a wayward child. Remember that God, the perfect Father, has more than a few wayward children. Let that soak in for a moment.

God gave His children everything they could possibly need in the garden. They had everything a person could want or imagine. The Creator walked with them and talked with them. He laughed with them and gave them all the love and provision they needed. Yet, they chose to believe the lies of the serpent over all that God had given them. They chose the path of death and destruction.

Ultimately, our children and grandchildren make their own choices throughout their lives. Yet, when a child goes astray and makes really bad decisions, the questions persist. *Could I have been a better parent? Is all of this somehow my fault?* Feelings of guilt and shame are real, but are they justified? That's what we will examine next.

2

The Guilt-Blame Trap

In her book *Raising Your Children's Children*, Martha Evans Sparks tells of one couple's experience in a courtroom after being granted full custody of their grandchild.[1]

> The judge, dressed in a long black robe, every wave of his hair carefully in place, looked down from his high bench.
> "Are you this boy's grandparents?"
> "Yes, your honor—we are," said David.
> "I grant you custody of your grandchild." Looking at Margaret, he added, "Try to do a better job this time."

Wham! Talk about a blow to one's sense of worth and competence. It would not be difficult for any of us to imagine how that might have felt. In fact, I suspect what that judge said is a familiar message to many of you. Sadly, it is not just in the courtroom where an attempt to shame and blame may be played out. It may be a message you tell yourself. Perhaps you perceive a similar opinion from friends you know, or even from a family member.

During a conversation with a friend in a coffee shop about the struggle some grandparents were facing in this area of guilt—that somehow they were responsible for the choice their child made—I attempted to describe a particular situation with which I was personally familiar. His response was, "Maybe they are at fault. I have to wonder if their decision to take in those grandchildren is simply enabling that adult child to continue in her irresponsible ways." He even suggested that the grandparents were likely repeating decisions that led to the adult child's issues in the first place, implying that poor parenting skills were being repeated now as enabling grandparents.

I know situations like this are not uncharted territory to those who are painfully aware of an adult child's poor choices that have landed you in your particular situation. You notice the disapproving looks of others and the hurtful comments from other family members. If those aren't painful enough, *you* start to question your fitness as a parent. Maybe some of these people are right and you could end up making the same mistakes parenting this grandchild that you did with your own children. But that is fear-based thinking.

It is natural to have doubts and to question yourself when you have a wayward child. You are not alone in this. There are lots of Christian parents with wayward adult children. But the choices your child made in his or her life that led to your grandchildren being removed from their care ought not to define who you are, nor your ability to productively provide for those children.

We already discussed the fact that God, the perfect parent, has wayward children. If you made some parenting mistakes that you need to confess to your children, then do that. But beyond that, your children's decisions are their own and not your responsibility. I plead with you to quit allowing others, even if it is someone in a position of authority, to tell you otherwise. I urge you to listen to what God says, not what others presume to know.

So, what does God say? Plenty. Here are three crucial truths that, when you choose to believe them, have the power to release you from the need to absorb guilt and shame regarding your adult child's actions that do not belong to you. Your belief in these truths also frees you to provide a loving, healthy home for your grandchildren. If you do not believe these truths, you will find yourself in bondage to falsehoods from which Christ died to free you. For the sake of your grandchildren and your freedom to live in God's grace and peace, I urge you to embrace what the Bible says is true.

1. **You are not responsible for the sins of your children.** "The one who sins is the one who will die. The child will not share the guilt of the parent, nor will the parent share the guilt of the child. The righteousness of the righteous will be credited to them, and the wickedness of the wicked will be charged against them" (Ezekiel 18:20).

    You are not responsible for the decisions and choices your children or grandchildren make in life, *but you are responsible for the way you influence them.* If you influenced them negatively, then you most certainly bear responsibility for that. God asks you to own up to those sins, repent, and seek reconciliation.

    Please understand this is not an either-or situation—that you are either totally responsible for their bad choices, or you have no responsibility at all. It would be wrong to deny any responsibility for how your life has influenced them. God has made it clear that parents and grandparents *are* to be a strong influence in their upbringing and training. Your influence does impact them. If you were abusive and detached, then your influence most likely has had an impact on their choices, and you need to confess that. You may need to go to your child and ask their forgiveness. But, in the end, it is the individual who must choose how he or she will respond to all the influences in their life. Two people with the exact same influences (positive and negative) may make completely different choices. Even so, own up to the choices and actions for which you are responsible.

However, when it is all said and done, even the best parenting cannot guarantee the direction a child may choose to go. This true story illustrates what could be your story.

> When I was nineteen, I decided I'd be honest and stop saying I was a Christian. At first, I pretended that my reasoning was high-minded and philosophical. But really I just wanted to drink gallons of cheap sangria and sleep around. Four years of this and I was strung out, stupefied, and generally pretty low. Especially when I was sober or alone.
>
> My parents—strong believers who raised their kids as well as any parents I've ever seen—were brokenhearted and baffled. I'm sure they wondered why the child they tried to raise right was such a ridiculous screw-up now.[2]

This was written by Abraham Piper, son of John Piper, well-known pastor and author. You can be the best parent humanly possible and still have one or more children choose to ignore what you say and go a different direction. It is a choice they make, and it may never make any sense to you.

Let me say it again. We have influence upon our children for good or bad. We will be accountable to God for how we parent. Even so, your child is still responsible for the choices he or she makes. Every person will give account for what they do or don't do with what they were given—good or bad.

There are some, like the judge at the beginning of this chapter, who attempt to place all the blame for a child's actions on you. Ultimately, God will justly judge it all. Make sure you are doing the best you can according to God's instructions for being a positive, godly influence in your child's life. Own up to your mistakes, but do not let the enemy put guilt and shame where it does not belong.

2. **Shame and condemnation are the work of the Accuser.** "Your enemy, the devil, prowls around like a roaring lion looking for someone to devour" (1 Peter 5:8). One of his prime targets in his prowling about is the family. He would like nothing more than to feed you lies about you and your family. Before we proceed further on this matter, let me clarify what I mean when I use the word *shame*.

I'll start by addressing the kind of shame about which I am *not* referring. I am not speaking of justifiable shame that results from something terrible I have done that brings injury (physical, mental, emotional) upon others and attacks the character and grace of God. That is shame that we feel because we know we are guilty. It is the kind of shame that we ought to feel and allow to lead us into the grace and forgiveness of Christ.

There is, however, another kind of shame to which we must not fall prey. It is that which comes from the devil himself—a shame imposed upon you by others, not God. It is a shame that you choose to wear like a robe, believing

29

that you are unworthy and unfit, and that your child's decisions are proof of that. But the point of grace is that none of us are worthy, and that's why the gospel is good news.

By faith you accept the truth about who you are as a child of God—that He loves and places such high value on you, not because you deserve it, but because His love for you is so great. The good news is that what you could not do for yourself, God in His infinite love did for you in Christ. He paid the debt you could not pay and removed the shame of your sin with His own righteousness.

Self-inflicted or others-inflicted shame that makes a good parent believe God blames them for their child's choice comes from the Accuser. It is meant to paralyze and destroy. This kind of shame may be the fruit of unbelief— that you do not believe God is bigger than your mistakes, and that if your child went astray then it must be your fault.

This is the kind of shame that leads to self-condemnation. It is choosing to believe that your faults as a parent condemn your child to wrong choices and therefore you must bear the blame. What could be more effective for achieving Satan's objective of destroying the family than filling you with paralyzing condemnation? He knows that if he can destroy the family, he can also destroy a nation and make the church impotent. On the other hand, when you know the truth, the truth shall set you free. Which brings me to the third critical truth . . .

3. **Christ's sufficiency is the whole point of the gospel.** Let's assume you did some things as a parent that you regret. Is the blood of Christ sufficient for that, or does Christ's atonement cover only certain sins and not others? Redemption is about restoring what was lost and making it

new. The gospel is good news, not only because God has forgiven us and freed us from a deserved condemnation, but because God delights in redeeming what is broken and making it into something beautiful. This is the unexpected opportunity mentioned in the previous chapter.

God's grace is sufficient for all of that. In fact, when God would not remove some great thorn from the apostle Paul's life, even though he pled with Him to remove it, Paul took comfort in God's words: "My grace is sufficient for you, for my power is made perfect in weakness" (2 Corinthians 12:9). God's grace frees us from ourselves and our unbelief. Yes, the good news is that "there is now no condemnation for those who are in Christ Jesus" (Romans 8:1), but also that His grace is sufficient for you, even in this dark hour of your life.

Now that the truth that sets you free from all shame and condemnation is in the bank, you can take one more truth to the bank and deposit it. As a beloved child of God, clothed in Christ's righteousness, His love and peace are yours because His presence is with you always. He has given you His Spirit to be your Comforter and Helper (John 14:26–27 ESV), so that you might not be troubled, but rest in His peace.

This same God also promised never to leave you or forsake you because you are now His. This is not a contingent "if you will, I will" promise. You may distance yourself from God, but He will not forsake you. He is always pursuing and waiting. You can rest with complete confidence in His promise.

How does knowing all of this solve the daily reality of the rubble your wayward child has left in your lives and the lives of your grandchildren? The pain of that reality steals so much of the joy and peace you want to experience.

31

I am convinced God's Word speaks life-giving truth for every life situation and relationship. It is upon that foundation that we will journey together into a place of hope and blessing.

In the throes of the trials you are facing with your adult child or with the challenges of raising your grandchild, what do you believe about God? Do you believe He cares about you and your situation? How strong is your faith right now? That's what I want to talk about with you next.

3

When Faith Is Put to the Test

Why would God let this happen to us and our grandchildren? Does He even care about what we are going through? These are some of the questions Rachel had as she struggled to understand the sequence of events that were unfolding in her life. Rachel's story is probably similar to yours, and it is the reason this book needs to be written. Here is some of Rachel's story in her own words.

I think most grandparents would agree that even before your grandchild arrives, you are already deeply and completely in love with them. We were no different. I was head over heels when our first granddaughter, Amber, arrived. We were so grateful that she was healthy, even though she had a rough beginning.

Unfortunately, her mother struggled with drug addiction and was using at the beginning of her pregnancy. We were able to get her help and into rehab early on. We were praying that it would be enough to allow the baby to grow healthy and strong.

By God's grace, and our daughter's determination to remain sober, Amber arrived healthy. This was a day to rejoice.

However, my daughter's complications during labor resulted in a great deal of pain after delivery. The hospital, not knowing about her drug problem, gave her opioids for the pain. My daughter began a downward spiral. Shortly after coming home, she began asking me to take Amber overnight, then for the weekend. Suffering from postpartum depression, our daughter was soon leaving her with us for a week at a time. Before long, Social Services got involved.

Following a difficult series of events, my husband and I received custody of our granddaughter while my daughter reentered rehab. After numerous failed attempts by our daughter to maintain her sobriety, and long months of court hearings, the court felt it had no choice but to take away her parental rights. They decided it was time to find a permanent forever family for our granddaughter. It was a sad time for us, but we were already her family, and there was no way we were giving Amber over to the system. We decided to proceed with adoption.

Then, before we could wrap up the court proceedings, we discovered our daughter was expecting a second baby. Shock and worry overwhelmed our hearts. Again, we prayed for a healthy baby, and miraculously, God gave us a healthy and beautiful grandson. Just like what happened with the first grandbaby, my daughter and her boyfriend lost custody of their second child.

The whole family was in a state of mourning as we felt the loss. As her mother, I clung to the hope that they would be able to pull through, conquer their addictions, and get their son back. The court wanted to keep our grandson and granddaughter together as a sibling group, so we received custody of him as well. Unfortunately, my daughter and her boyfriend were unsuccessful in their efforts to follow through with the requirements of the court. As a result, we now have two adopted grandbabies.

As with any adoption, it began with trauma for the children—the trauma of being taken away from their parents; the trauma of being placed in our home; the trauma of starting over. The adjustment period was very difficult. Amber cried for hours on end every day for several months. She was diagnosed with reactive attachment disorder (RAD).

Her condition kept me inside and isolated for the first few months. I felt very alone and disconnected from my world. At times I experienced overwhelming sadness. It all seemed more than I could bear. Did God see me? Did He know what we were going through? Did He care for my daughter's heart while I couldn't be with her? So many heart-wrenching questions and very few answers. I was losing my joy. Sometimes I thought I was losing my mind.

Do Rachel's questions feel familiar to you? I suspect they are questions that resonate with you on a very tender soul level. I pray earnestly that you will believe and know how much God cares and sees your struggle. Unless you believe that, your questions only serve as empty reminders of doubt that will keep you from knowing God's grace in full measure.

Even though the apostle Paul did not have grandchildren, he knew what it was to suffer and feel deep pain, both physically and relationally. He also knew that those who put their trust in God would have that trust tested. Knowing that would be the case, he shared how he prayed for any believer enduring difficult circumstances. These are prayers we ought to be praying too. These are my prayers for you.

A Prayer for Wisdom with a Purpose

I keep asking that the God of our Lord Jesus Christ, the glorious Father, may give you the Spirit of wisdom and *revelation, **so that you may know him better**. I pray also that the eyes of your heart may be enlightened in order that **you may know the hope to which he has called you**, the riches of his glorious inheritance in his holy people, and **his incomparably great power for us who believe**. (Ephesians 1:17–19, emphasis added)*

Did you catch the first objective of Paul's prayer—"Give you the Spirit of wisdom and revelation, so that you may know [God] better" (v. 17)? Let me ask you a critical question. What do you believe about God? Do you believe He wants what is best for you, your grandchildren, and your family? I'm serious. This is a vital question, because what you believe about God and His heart for those He called to himself is everything. He doesn't call you to himself so that He can make your life miserable. What I'm asking has nothing to do with what you *say* you believe, but whether you truly believe it.

That's important because we do what we believe. We may not always do what we profess, but we will do what we believe. If you believe God takes pleasure in your suffering, you will have little interest in knowing Him or believing He is good.

On the other hand, if you believe God is good and desires what is best, you will work hard to cultivate that spirit of wisdom and revelation in which knowing God's heart is your objective. When you do, God will reveal himself to you in powerful ways. Often, it is in our darkest moments that He reveals himself most clearly.

Notice, too, that Paul's prayer is not only for a spirit of wisdom and revelation but also that our eyes will be enlightened to the truth about the hope to which He has called us—even in this difficult time. Hope can never endure if it is based upon circumstances. It must always be focused in Him who has promised us a glorious inheritance **yet to come**, accomplished through His incomparably great power **right now** to those who believe. What do you believe about God's power to fulfill this promise for you? Paul's prayer is that your eyes would be enlightened to His "incomparably great power for us **who believe**."

Another apostle, Peter, makes this bold statement: "His divine power has given us everything we need for a godly life through our knowledge of him who has called us by his own glory and goodness" (2 Peter 1:3). He has already given us **everything** we need to persevere and overcome whatever has been dealt us. In Him we have no deficiencies for life. Do you believe that?

As Paul prayed for believers in his day, I also pray this for you, that you will have a spirit of wisdom to know Him who knows you fully, and that you will experience the joyous hope and peace that come through His promises to you. I pray your heart will be so gloriously enlightened to that hope for both eternity and today that you will experience the power He provides to strengthen you in the face of anything life throws at you. And I pray you will do so with the confidence that His grace is sufficient.

A Prayer for Discernment

*And this is my prayer: that your love may abound more and more in knowledge and depth of insight, so **that you may be able to discern what is best** and may be pure and blameless until the day of Christ, filled with the fruit of righteousness that comes through Jesus Christ—to the glory and praise of God. (Philippians 1:9–11, emphasis added)*

Discernment is not always recognizable when you are in the middle of something with which you have a strong emotional connection. But neither is it elusive. That's why Paul offers this prayer to those of us seeking to understand what to do when confusion and stress consume us. He knows that discernment is essential for making good decisions and sticking by them. But his prayer for discernment is rooted in a critical assumption: that our love will abound more and more. In other words, the key for unlocking godly discernment is loving well. Let me try to unpack what that looks like.

Love is not static. For human beings, it is constantly changing. Our love grows or shrinks according to our depth of insight. Only God's love is perfect and unchangeable. Like a plant, love needs constant watering to keep growing and remain healthy. If it doesn't get the water it needs, it shrivels up. So, how do we "water" love?

Notice that Paul is praying that our love "abound more and more in *knowledge and depth of insight*." He is saying that the keys to a love that abounds, love that flourishes and overflows, are not feelings or determination, but two often forgotten factors—knowledge and insight. How does that work?

1. **Knowledge is the watering can for love.** Love is a motivation for knowledge, but it is also the fruit of knowledge. For example, when I first met my wife, Diane, what I knew about her made me want to know more and more about her. As I learned more about her, I realized how much I loved her, and the more I knew, the more my love grew. Now, after fifty years, you would think I would know all I could possibly know about her. But that's not so. I'm still learning, and my love is still growing and abounding, especially when I see how she's loved me with all my flaws.

2. **Depth of insight is something more than mere knowledge.** It is about discernment. I knew Diane was attractive and

fun to be around. I knew some of her skills and inter-
ests. But those characteristics by themselves were not the
impetus for my love growing and flourishing. It was a
deepening insight into what I knew about her. I learned
what made her tick and the character underneath all the
external qualities I observed. As my insight into who she
really was deepened, so did my love.

It's the same with our love for the Lord. Remember the first
prayer we examined in Ephesians? The spirit of wisdom and
revelation is for the purpose of knowing God better. But this
knowing is more than what's in my head. I know God is great
and almighty. I know He is sovereign and majestic. But do I
know why those facts about God matter? Do I know His goodness and grace in ways that make His character clear and give
me a reason to both love and trust Him? Do I recognize the
evidence of His love in both the good times and the bad?

Knowledge of the Father and the Son, combined with depth
of insight, leads to increased love for God and others. Here's
my interpretation of what Paul is saying: "Look, I am praying
your love will overflow because you choose to know God better every day. The more you know who He really is, the more
you love Him, and the more you love Him, the more you know
that what He desires is best for you and those you love. The
very things that make Him so amazing and loving also bring
glory and praise to Him—and He is worthy of all that praise."

So, let's circle back to the question of discernment in Paul's
prayer. Our measure of knowledge and depth of insight into
the character and attributes of God gives us what we need to
discern what are the most pure and blameless choices in life.
The Father is delighted to hear us ask for discernment when
we don't know what to do.

However, discernment is not limited to good choices and decisions. Discernment that is pure and good does not originate in the head or the heart but in God's Word. It springs from our love and trust in God. Otherwise, it becomes empty and devoid of compassion—and therefore useless. True discernment emanates from a relationship with God that is continually growing through our knowledge of Him.

I believe knowledge and depth of insight are directly related. The more you know the Father's heart, the more understanding you will gain for what to do in everyday circumstances. Scripture, prayer, and relationships with fellow believers are our tools for knowing Him more. We were designed that way—members of one another as the body of Christ. On our own, we are removed from the life-giving relationships in which each member is doing their part to build up one another in love and maturity.

Paul prayed this prayer in Philippians because of his confidence in God to complete the work He had already begun in them (v. 6). Now, out of his affection for them, he wants their love to grow so they can discern what is best and apply it in all of their relationships to the glory of God, no matter how hard life is.

My prayer for you is that your love will grow so much that your home will become a sanctuary of love that reflects Jesus's love to all. Submerge yourself in the Word and the fellowship of God's people so you may stimulate one another to love and good deeds demonstrated by Jesus as He revealed the Father's love. When we love like Christ, love abounds, and discernment also abounds. And where there is discernment, there is also blessing expressed through the fruit of righteous actions and decisions.

I know you may be weary and overwhelmed, but I urge you to remember that Jesus calls you to come to Him and learn from Him and He will give you rest. Do not allow yourself to believe such rest is not available to you. Choose the better way. Your faith will be tested in this, so do not lose heart. Here are two suggestions to help you find that rest.

1. **Learn the practice of praying without ceasing.** Maybe you can't always find a regular moment for a true quiet time. But you can pray while you're dealing with a crying child or a hectic schedule. Jesus never said you had to come to Him in a quiet garden setting. He just said to come, and that means even when you are overwhelmed by burdensome moments. "They that wait upon the LORD [even in chaotic moments] shall renew their strength . . . they shall run, and not be weary; and they shall walk, and not faint" (Isaiah 40:31 KJV).

   I heard it once said that

   > If we depend on organizations, then we will get what organizations have to give;
   > If we depend on education (or intellect), then we will get what education has to give;
   > If we depend on men or military might, then we will get what men and military might have to give;
   > *If we depend upon prayer, then we will get what God has to give.*

2. **Trust in the sovereignty of God, even when it seems like it is more than you can bear.** This is another point of faith testing. Do you believe God when He says "all things God works for the good of those who love him, who have been called according to his purpose" (Romans 8:28)? Tell Him you don't understand but that you trust Him because He understands what is best.

There is much more potential for rest in trusting than in worrying and fretting.

Here's something I've found helpful when faced with this matter of trust in the midst of hard times. I look back at another particularly difficult time in my life when it seemed that there could not possibly be anything good that could come from that situation. I remember how much I lacked in the trust department, but then I smile when I remember the good that God brought about through it—with great pain to be sure, but also with great blessing in the long run.

When Moses presented all the reasons why he was not the right person to deliver God's people from slavery, God's response to him probably caught Moses off guard. God did not respond to Moses's excuses or feelings of inadequacy. He simply said this: "I AM WHO I AM. This is what you are to say to the Israelites: 'I AM has sent me to you'" (Exodus 3:14).

In other words, God told Moses it doesn't matter who you are, what your résumé says, or what your circumstances are. This is a test of your faith. What God told Moses also applies to you. Here it is: "I AM (My Presence) is with you. You are not alone. That is enough because my grace is sufficient, and my power is made perfect in your weakness!"

And here's some really good news! The One who is with us understands. We do not have a High Priest (Jesus) who is unable to sympathize with our sufferings. He knows the pain you are experiencing. He knows how hard it is to be doing what you are doing. Our Savior knows what it is to be totally rejected and alone. He who understands is with you.

I know what is going on now is not what you planned for your family. Yet, for some reason, God has given you an opportunity to grow in wisdom, love, and faith. Where wisdom and love abound, the seeds of righteousness will bear much fruit in you and your family. I pray your hope will be strengthened because you know Him better and are abounding in the love with which He loves you. I pray that God will give you great endurance, insight, and patience through His divine power so that you will know what is best and find grace in your time of need.

4

You Keep Using That Word

Bob and Valerie deeply loved their grandchildren even before they knew anything about Christ's love. They fully embraced the unexpected task of raising three grandsons (ages four, five, and six). It fell to them because their youngest daughter made some very poor choices in her life, resulting in her giving birth to three boys each by a different father. She and the boys lived in their home until she decided to move in with a new boyfriend—one more bad decision. Tragically, within a month, their daughter was brutally murdered by that boyfriend.

Bob and Valerie found themselves in the midst of a nightmare, searching for answers. On the way to the funeral home for a viewing, four-year-old Stephin said, "We don't have to see Mommy. She's not there. She's with my friend."

They had no idea who he was talking about, but when they arrived at the funeral home, Stephin saw an artist's rendering of Jesus and said, "That's my friend." That conversation and the pastor's message at the funeral launched them on a journey that would change their lives.

The pastor who performed the funeral had earlier knocked on their door after hearing about the tragic incident with their daughter. He simply wanted to come by and offer any comfort or assistance he could provide. Because of that visit, Bob and Valerie asked him to speak at the funeral. He accepted without any expectation about their coming to his church. The pastor's sincere compassion, moving message, and nonintrusive manner opened the door for them to want to check out his church.

For the first time, they heard the gospel and experienced a kind of love they had not known before. In this church, they found friends who were gracious and giving. They found both a safe place to process their grief and a transformational renewal through the gospel. This was where they belonged. This was now their family.

Funny thing about how we talk about love (actually, it's not so funny). It is one of those words we glibly throw around with as many different meanings and nuances as a politician's promises. No matter how many diluted meanings we may assign to this important word, Jesus was very clear about the weight of a word we often misunderstand.

One of the last things Jesus communicated to His disciples before going to the cross was a new command—the foundation of the new covenant that would be sealed by His own blood: "My command is this: Love each other as I have loved you. Greater love has no one than this: to lay down one's life for one's friends" (John 15:12-13).

I know you love your grandchildren with all your heart. The fact that you have taken them into your care and sacrificed so much for their well-being is proof of that. You are living examples of a laying-down-your-life kind of love.

But what about other family members, those who do not look as kindly on your decisions? How about those people who pass judgment on your parenting skills? Or that wayward child who has caused you so much pain and continues to deposit a pile of debris in your life? What does that do to the way you think of God's love for you and how He cares about your situation? Do you understand the impact the gospel ought to have on how you view God's love and how you love Him?

Bob and Valerie will tell you today that embracing the gospel and being part of a church family has changed everything. It's been a hard journey for them, but they have learned the importance of a faith family. In Christ and the family of God they found the strength to press on during the hard times, to grow personally, and to trust that God is working in all for their good and the good of their grandchildren.

They also discovered the power of Christ's love to transform their home and the way they love. As Bob says, "We know we must make sure the grandchildren (now adopted) know they are loved by us and by Christ. They also need to know how much their mother is loved. We think every parent who has an adult child incapable of taking care of their own children ought to express their love for that child. Just because they are incapable of being a parent does not mean they are not loved. We are committed to express that love and respect because that is how God and the church love us."

Your story may be very different from Bob and Valerie's story. Your grandchildren may not have lost their mom or dad to a horrible murder or a car accident. But they have lost their parent(s) to something just as awful—drugs, imprisonment, or some other tragic event. Your grandchildren are forced to grow up without their biological parent or parents, and, even if it is only temporary, it is still traumatic.

Bob and Valerie received lots of community support and encouragement because of the circumstances of their tragedy. You may not have experienced that kind of outpouring of support and assistance. In fact, you may have experienced more sideways glances and questions about your parenting than compassion and encouragement.

Despite your circumstances, this same love Bob and Valerie have experienced and are able to offer can change everything for you as it did for them. In Christ, you have been shown the kind of love you are now able to offer your family. You chose to be the parent your adult children cannot be. There was never any doubt about it in your mind. Your grandchildren belong to you.

At the same time, doubts may linger—not about your love for them, but about whether your love is strong enough to overcome feelings of anger, angst, and unworthiness. Do you have what it takes to love your adult child the way he or she ought to be loved? It's one thing to love your grandchild as the victim, but are you capable of another kind of love for that wayward child who has hurt you and your grandchildren so deeply?

Another of Jesus's last statements to His disciples before He went to the cross was this: "A new command I give you: Love one another. As I have loved you, so you must love one another. By this everyone will know that you are my disciples, if you love one another" (John 13:34–35). He repeated this later that evening when He said, "My command is this: Love each other as I have loved you" (John 15:12).

This was important to Jesus, and He wanted to make sure the disciples understood how important it was. He had come to fulfill the law of the old covenant through His own death. On the cross He paid the sin debt we could not pay ourselves—a debt not even the temple sacrificial system could pay. Something new was about to happen that the disciples did not yet grasp.

The old law only served to expose the horrid sinfulness of our hearts and the great offense that our sin is to a holy, righteous God. Jesus would be the perfect, final sacrifice for those offenses. He would establish a new law in a new kingdom in which we would become the temple where the Father resided through His Holy Spirit. By Jesus's righteousness, we stand before Almighty God redeemed and cleansed of our sin.

As a result, we are free to have our focus be on loving God and one another as Christ has loved us. When Jesus gave this new command to the disciples, He knew loving one another would not be an easy task. No one is easy to love all the time, and sometimes our notion of what love looks like can be skewed. But Jesus did not sit above us in heaven and hand down an impossible edict without showing us how it can be done.

He came to us in total humility. He laid aside His divine glory and lived among us to show what love looks like by serving— not being served. Then He demonstrated the ultimate expression of love by giving himself as a ransom for we who were not worthy of His love. When Jesus said, "Greater love has no man than this, that he lay down his life for his friends [or family]," He proved it by doing it on the cross.

Now He turns to all of us and asks us to obey His new command: *Love one another as I have loved you.* This is the other kind of love that you are being asked to teach and express to your grandchildren and to those adult children who made poor choices and mistakes that have brought you all to this place. It is the kind of love that only exists in the context of the transformational work of the gospel in which God's grace given by faith in Christ makes us alive to love as Christ loves us.

What does that look like? I'm going to step out on a limb and offer six ways I think loving as Christ loves looks like in your circumstances:

1. **Believe that what you are doing is God's best for this situation.** (We've come back to Romans 8:28 from Chapter 2). Senator Collins, co-sponsor of the Supporting Grandparents Raising Grandchildren Act, is right when she says you are "replacing traumatic pasts with loving and hopeful futures."[1] This is one of the grand and good works God is accomplishing in your grandchildren's lives through you. You must never lose sight of that. God has placed you in this place of caring for your grandchild(ren) to work all things for good—to show your grandchildren God's redeeming love and grace in the midst of a cursed and broken world. Perhaps God is using this to change the heart of your son or daughter as well.

2. **See your grandchild(ren) through a parent's eyes.** Love them as a parent more than a grandparent. I know there are times when you just want to be a grandparent without all the responsibilities of a parent. That isn't your prerogative right now, and it isn't fair. I think we can agree on that. There's nothing wrong with wanting to relate to them as your grandchildren, but you must accept that you are the only parent they have right now. Be cautious about blurring those lines.

   For this reason, I offer one caveat about your relationship with your grandchildren: Loving your grandchildren does not equate with pampering them or doting on them. (By the way, this is true whether you're raising them or not!) Love does not ignore the responsibility we have to train up a child in the way he or she should go. They need to know they are loved, and that you love them too much to allow them to run the show. You are not their BFF!

   Children need parents who love them and are willing to do the hard work of teaching and training them. Love is not afraid of doing the hard things. Saying "no" may be one of those hard things, if it is for their good. Isn't that the whole objective of love—the very best for the one we love? Guard yourself from the temptation to slip into taking the easy way out and miss what is in their best interest.

3. **Don't see yourself as their savior.** These children are bringing emotional baggage with them, and much of it may be beyond what you think you can bear. Don't assume it's your responsibility to fix what's broken. You aren't a failure when you admit what you cannot do. Seek help for the sake of the children, but seek it wisely. Ask people you trust to help you with this process, including your church.

4. **Keep mealtime a family priority.** I know your schedules are crazy, and your physical capacities are not the same as they were when you were a young parent. Even so, I plead with you to protect the family table. It is one of the most important places for doing life together in a very powerful way. Make this a time for transparency and exploring life's questions together—a place where they feel safe to share hurts and doubts, where they know they are loved as they are.

5. **Establish a spoken blessing as a consistent practice in your family.** Your grandchildren are a precious treasure from God and to God. They have probably experienced plenty of cursing in their young lives. They desperately need to hear words of blessing and encouragement from you. Make it a regular practice to praise them, not just for things they have done, but for who they are. We'll take a deeper look at the spoken blessing in Chapter 6.

6. **Keep your heart turned toward God.** The best way you can love your grandchildren as Christ loved us is to love God

with all your being. There is nothing you want more for your grandchildren than that they find new life in Christ. While you can't make that decision for them, when your life shouts that Christ is your all-satisfying delight, they will notice and it will impact them.

A heart after God is a heart shaped by the gospel. You love because He first loved you. Stay in the Word, but also stay on your knees. Do not neglect friendship with like-minded followers of Christ who will encourage you, exhort you, and challenge you in your daily walk. When your love for God is strong, your love for your family will be strong.

It really is about first things first, isn't it? The Bible says it will be the righteous who flourish and bear fruit even in old age. Grandpa and Grandma, this means you. Bearing fruit and flourishing is the mark of those who first seek God and His reign, even in old age. They are the ones who will love well and proclaim to those who follow the truth that God is trustworthy, all-powerful, sovereign, and faithful. So, seek Him first!

5

You Can't Give
What You Do Not Have

Sherry and her husband, Steve, have fostered four and adopted one of their grandchildren. Not only are they now raising their grandchild, but, as an advocate, she is heavily involved in helping more than one hundred other grandparents who are also raising their grandchildren—most with very limited means. It's a big task, one that would overwhelm a lesser person.

Sherry knows firsthand what it's like to experience those dark clouds of discouragement that arise when you're feeling overwhelmed. She would also tell you about an important factor that can open the door to despair and allow a sense of hopelessness to overtake you when things are hard.

"The very last thing a mother or grandmother may do is take care of herself," Sherry confesses. "Most never think about how important that is."

Does that sound familiar to you? Perhaps you are uncomfortable with attending to your own well-being because it feels selfish and self-centered. After all, God gave you the task of caring for these precious grandchildren. Whether you asked for it or not, you have embraced this opportunity to provide what they need. Your needs come second.

I commend you for your commitment, yet is it possible that neglecting to care for yourself could actually hinder your ability to fully care for your grandchildren? I know self-care sounds so, well, self-centered. And in a real sense, modern psychology's focus on self-improvement and self-empowerment is self-centered. Does that mean self-care is unbiblical?

The Bible does have a great deal to say about care, but not in the same way modern self-care practitioners talk about it. I think blogger Joanna Mikhail hits the nail on the head when she says that "we are created to rest in God. When I understood this, I realized that 'biblical self-care' isn't *self*-care at all, it is surrender to divine care."[1]

So, what does it mean to surrender to divine care? The answer begins with two questions. First, what do you believe about God, how He created us, and His instructions about personal care? Second, what do you believe the Bible says about your part in the process? If you don't believe God takes it seriously and has provided instructions for your personal care, you won't take it seriously. The truth is you cannot give what you do not have, and what you need only God can give.

Obviously, God created our bodies to respond positively to healthy food, sleep, and physical exercise, and likewise our minds to information, communication (relationships), and wise counsel. We all engage in these things with varying degrees of intentionality, and yet there is one thing we must remember. You and I have nothing to do with the outcome. That is solely God's work as the Designer. Ours is merely to apply the conditions of His design for the desired results. But apply them we must if we want to be healthy and productive.

This is true for our soul as well. As the seat of our spiritual health, our souls bear the image of God breathed into us by our Creator. Like the body and mind, the care of our soul requires intentionality according to God's biblical instructions. The attention we give to these instructions will impact our soul, which impacts our effectiveness as spiritual influencers in our grandchildren's lives. If I do not intentionally care for my soul, there will be negative consequences in my ability to proclaim Christ to those whom God calls me to influence.

So, let's be sure we're clear about two critical truths that define this matter of caring for both body and soul:

1. God is the sole *author* of our need for personal rest and care (physically and spiritually) and the sole *provider* of that care. When we surrender to His care as He designed it, there is life and contentment—what we often refer to as *well-being*.

   Modern self-empowerment and self-awareness techniques that focus on *self* contradict what Jesus says. He declares that the key to saving your life is not "finding yourself," but "denying yourself" (Mark 8:34–36). It is foolish and dangerous to believe that I am the key to my own well-being. Which brings us to the second truth . . .

2. Our personal care is activated through our surrender to God's divine care plan. This surrender is not passive, but an intentional course of action according to the Father's design for our good and His glory. To better understand what that looks like, let's take a look at Psalm 23.

What More Could I Want?

I recently visited the Grand Canyon with one of my grandsons. We walked the Rim Trail, where we encountered numerous overlook points, each offering a unique vista and perspective of the canyon and God's wondrous handiwork. It is an indescribable experience but easy to miss the significance of it if you do not have eyes to see.

The Twenty-third Psalm is like a Grand Canyon vista of God's glory and goodness. It will change your perspective . . . if you have eyes to see. So, pause with me at four key overlooks to gaze upon a wondrous landscape of God's goodness, His wondrous design for your soul's rest.

At this first overlook, we can observe the nature and breadth of the Shepherd's care, the Source of our rest and hope.

Overlook #1: The Shepherd

David wrote this psalm knowing a lot about shepherding and sheep because he was once a shepherd. Yet, interestingly, he did not write Psalm 23 from the perspective of the shepherd, but of the sheep—a sheep's view of the Lord as his shepherd, who is a better shepherd than David ever was. He wrote to remind us how much we need a shepherd and the extraordinary goodness this Shepherd places in our stories.

The Lord is my shepherd; I shall not want (v. 1 esv). Perhaps a four-year-old's version of this verse really does capture the essence of it: "The Lord is my shepherd; **what more could I want!**" I think she nailed it. This Shepherd is the cause of, the reason for, and the motivation behind all that follows in this psalm. This better Shepherd is our Lord, our King, our

Savior—the One who meets all our needs. What else could we want?

To be sure, not all shepherds attend well to the sheep in their care. But this Shepherd is different. He is the Good Shepherd who attends to every need of His sheep. And sheep are needy. In fact, of all living animals, sheep are among the most helpless and dependent on the planet (though I doubt if you asked the sheep they would agree).

Regardless of how most sheep think, this sheep (David) knows he needs a shepherd, and what better shepherd could he have than the Lord? He's not just the shepherd of a large nameless flock, but He is *my* shepherd. He knows *my* name, this lump of clay linked to the Divine Majesty. It is an intimacy that permits me to declare with David, "the LORD is **my** shepherd"—what Phillip Keller calls "a cherished object of divine diligence."[2]

What a thought to ponder! You are so cherished by your Creator that He has committed himself to your well-being. Can you see yourself so precious to the Lord as to lay claim to Him as *your* Shepherd? Do you believe this to be true?

Young Cory believed it, even knowing he was dying from cancer. His mother taught him to speak the Twenty-third Psalm using the five fingers of one hand to recite the first verse: "the LORD is my shepherd." As he spoke the word *my*, she had him grasp his ring finger in his fist and hold it tightly to symbolize the importance of that personal relationship with the Shepherd. Sadly, the disease took his life while he was still very young. His mother found him holding his ring finger with his fist. He died in the Shepherd's arms.

Jesus is your Shepherd. He opens His arms to you so all your wants may be satisfied in Him. What else could you want? Hold tightly to this truth.

Overlook #2: Provision and Preparation

My Shepherd's care is both nourishing and restorative. It is filled with good, nourishing provisions that feed my soul, compassionate actions that restore my soul, and guidance that keeps me on track. All of this the Shepherd provides. Perhaps, this is a good place to linger and learn how the Shepherd does this.

He makes me lie down in green pastures (v. 2). This is not a forceful action by the shepherd to coerce the sheep into a prone position. "Lie down, you dumb sheep!" On the contrary, it is a loving and gentle invitation. "Come to me, all you who are weary and burdened, and I will give you rest" (Matthew 11:28).

The pasture is available. He beckons us to come and be refreshed in a place of waiting and safety. Here you can turn away from the worries of life and ruminate on the goodness and graciousness of *your* Shepherd. It is an invitation the Shepherd continually offers, yet one we often find excuses for ignoring.

"But I am raising my young grandchildren. Where am I to find time for solitude?" You're right. It is hard. It's also hard for those who are not raising grandchildren. Yet Jesus does not issue impossible invitations. Those with heavy burdens and those who labor nonstop are those for whom His invitation is meant. You don't have to figure it out. You have only to *lie down*.

One overwhelmed mother believed it so important that she did it under a blanket. She instructed her children that when Mommy covered herself with her blanket, no one was to bother her. There would be no questions for Mommy, no demands of Mommy, no tugs on Mommy's blanket until she came out. This was Mommy's time alone with Jesus.

The invitation is real. You must decide if you will accept it—which means you have to believe it is important enough to use some blanket creativity. It is your choice. The invitation stands, and it is for your good.

He leads me beside still waters (v. 2b ESV). Sheep get thirsty. Our souls get thirsty, and the only thing that will quench that thirst is Christ, who knows where to find *still* waters.

He knows that the roaring waters of fast-moving rivers create anxiety for His sheep. He also knows that if a sheep's thirst is not satisfied, they will wander in search of other water sources, even if they are polluted. He also knows how to lead us to those *still waters* that quench our thirst.

In biblical language, drinking suggests the idea of "taking in" or "believing." Again, the invitation of the Shepherd is to *come*. He invites you to take in and believe that practices like meditating upon the Word and praying with a listening heart so you can know Him better, will satisfy your thirsty soul.

What are you willing to do to satisfy your thirst? The Shepherd leads us to the pure, still waters of His Word and prayer, but we must drink. Jesus promises that when we do, something remarkable and supernatural happens—"rivers of living water will flow from within" (John 7:38).

He restores my soul (v. 3 ESV). Sometimes even healthy sheep experience trouble. In the language of shepherds, it is the problem of "cast" sheep.

Cast sheep are usually healthy and content. Their wool is thick and long, but that state of comfort can also make them susceptible to carelessness. A sheep with heavy wool may lie down in a low spot in the pasture and roll back to get comfortable, only to find itself unable to get to its feet because it is weighed down.

This is what is meant by *cast* or *cast down* sheep. If not discovered by the shepherd quickly, a cast sheep can die within hours. A cast sheep is also very susceptible to predators, especially if it has wandered away from the flock. Speaking from the perspective of a sheep, David knew the dangers of a cast condition. We need to be aware of them too.

The first danger is forgetting how much the accumulation of difficult circumstances can weigh us down. Things pile up and pile up, and we do not realize the toll it is taking on our souls. The second danger is when we make choices that may feel more comfortable and offer some relief but put us in a dangerous position that is not good for the soul.

Consider, for example, when we stay away from church because it is too hard and people won't understand what we're going through. We forget how much we need one another because we are all part of the body of Christ. When we make those choices, we place ourselves in the same "cast down" condition as the cast sheep. Eventually we find ourselves on our own, vulnerable to the spiritual attack and isolation from those who can help.

This may be why David wrote in another psalm, "Search me, God, and know my heart; test me and know my anxious thoughts. See if there is any offensive way in me, and **lead me** in the way everlasting" (Psalm 139:23–24, emphasis added). This is the work the Spirit wants to do in us—search and lead. Ours is to let Him and then do what He asks us to do.

He leads me in paths of righteousness (v. 3b ESV). This is a grand perspective of the Shepherd's personal preparations that lead to paths of righteousness—**for His name's sake**. Once again, we come full circle to what all of this is about: It's about the Shepherd—His provisions for feeding and restoring our souls and His guidance to prepare us for whatever life may throw at us. It has nothing to do with self-empowerment or intellectual prowess. It is about our submission to the One who meets every need and to whom all praise belongs.

In his letter to the Ephesian church, Paul reminds us that the objective of our salvation is not just eternal life, but **good works** God prepared for us to do as His workmanship (Ephesians 2:10 ESV, emphasis added). These are the paths of righteousness. We walk the paths of righteousness by doing good works for His name's sake. These are the paths that make much of His name and His reputation in the eyes of those who know us.

Now we turn our attention to the final two overlooks, where David shifts from talking *about* the Lord, his Shepherd, to talking *to* Him directly. It is a grand overview of how the Shepherd is at work preparing us for the realities of a broken world. These realities are not unique to us—God's people have always had to learn to cope with a world filled with evil. David reminds us how blessed we are to have a Shepherd who both supplies everything we need for the well-being of our souls and continually comforts us through His presence as we face the challenges of life and look toward His grand purpose.

6

Shepherd-Driven Soul Care

The views from the first two overlooks of Psalm 23 reveal key foundational truths about caring for my soul, which are vital to having a godly influence in the lives of my grandchildren, whether I am raising them or not.

We learned that care is not self-driven, but Shepherd-driven. I have a Shepherd—*my* Shepherd—who is able to meet every need, restore my soul, and lead me in the way I should go. It has nothing to do with me and everything to do with Him. What else could I want but to surrender myself to Him?

Now we turn our attention to the two remaining overlooks. David draws us into the intimate relationship we enjoy with the Shepherd that is revealed in how we express our confident trust and genuine joy in Him.

Overlook #3: Protection

I remember as a child my dad taking me and my brother camping in a very special place in Wyoming. It was called Vedauwoo, and it had mountains of gigantic granite boulders that were paradise for young boys to explore and climb. However, when nightfall came, Vedauwoo was a frightening place for young boys. The shadows cast by the moon and the howls of coyotes in the distance were significant deterrents for leaving the safety of the campfire, even though I needed to visit the outhouse.

The outhouse seemed like a long way from the campsite. You had to walk down a gravel road, cross a small stream surrounded by an aspen grove, and walk between more granite boulders. But my father knew it was a trip that was absolutely necessary.

So he'd take the old Coleman lantern in one hand, take my hand in the other, and walk with me to the outhouse while humming or singing an old Disney tune: "O, the Lord is good to me . . ." I remember in that moment I felt safe, even though it was still a scary place. In my father's hand, with him singing over me in the dark, I knew I was safe.

It's like that with our heavenly Father. Whether dealing with the painful realities of our own mortality, fears within, or the enemy without, His presence is enough to sustain us through all of it. As the psalmist sees it, the Shepherd is our victory because of His presence and sacrifice.

*Even though I walk through the valley of the shadow of death, I will fear no evil, **for you are with me** . . .* (v. 4 ESV, emphasis added). The shepherd knows that the best route to the lush, high mountain meadows is through the valleys. In the valleys, the shepherd knows there is clean, refreshing water and the best grasses. But it is also in the dark valleys that predators lurk alongside other unforeseen dangers. There the fear of death is real. The Good Shepherd knows these things, but He also knows the journey through the valley is still the best route, and

His constant presence with the sheep provides both protection and freedom from fear.

Your rod and your staff, they comfort me (v. 4b). The shepherd's rod is an effective tool for defending against predators and for prodding the sheep to keep moving or avoid dangerous situations. The staff is used by the shepherd to both guide and rescue a wayward sheep from disaster by lifting it out of danger and back into the safety of the shepherd's arms.

Your Shepherd is constantly with you. He does not promise to eliminate the dark valleys and difficult paths in life, but He does promise to lead you through them. I will fear no evil because my Shepherd is with me, and His rod and staff do indeed bring me comfort. May you know the comfort and peace the Shepherd alone can give.

You prepare a table before me in the presence of my enemies (v. 5). A good shepherd spends an enormous amount of time preparing the mountain pastures (also known as *tables* or *mesas*) each spring before the sheep arrive. He goes to great lengths and personal sacrifice to make sure the pastures are ready and safe for his sheep. Perhaps this is what David envisioned as he wrote this part of the psalm.

I imagine he may also have foreseen that great banquet table of another Shepherd whom God promised would come after him. In David's use of the table metaphor, he suddenly shifts from shepherd imagery to king imagery. This is a king's banquet table prepared specifically for those who are His. It is a place of honor and favor, and it is intentionally held where our enemies will see. It is prepared for you—a place where the Shepherd King celebrates you and honors you with the anointing of oil fit for royalty.

It is also a place where you and I share an overflowing cup with the King at His table. Our Shepherd King has gone to great lengths to prepare His banquet table for us, even to the point of laying down His life for ours (Revelation 19:7–9). It is a cup symbolizing God's overflowing love and grace through the shed blood of Christ for our blessing and benefit. He has done the work on our behalf. We have only to remember His presence and receive His gracious provision that secures us against the fear of all evil. He does, after all, have our hand in His, and He is singing over us in the dark.

Overlook #4: The Promise

Before going to the cross, Jesus, our Good Shepherd, instructed the disciples to bear much fruit. But they could do so only if they learned to *abide* in Him. This is the whole point and purpose of Psalm 23—that abiding in the Shepherd's rest not only produces fruitful righteousness but also describes that which follows those who walk it. The idea of goodness and mercy following me all the days of my life is not a promise that plenty of sunshine is headin' my way . . . zip-a-dee-doo-dah! On the contrary, Jesus made it very clear we would have trouble in this world, "But take heart! I [Jesus] have overcome the world!" (John 16:33).

The Good Shepherd knows how to lead us down paths of righteousness, through valleys filled with shadows of death, and into lush green pastures with still waters. His care is sufficient for every situation, and when I surrender to that care, something in me is changed. His goodness and His mercy cover the trail I have walked.

We all know people who display little goodness or mercy in their lives. The trail that follows them is a trail of debris—anger, resentment, selfishness, and ruined relationships. Not so for those who have surrendered themselves to the care of the Good Shepherd. When we give ourselves over to the Shepherd's goodness and mercy, a trail of goodness and mercy will be evident to others. His goodness, His love, His mercy changes us, and changed people lead changed lives. It is a life with impact—what we call *legacy*.

In Moses's final sermon to the Israelites, he reminded them how faithful God had proved himself to them throughout their forty-year sojourn. Moses sternly warned them of the consequences of failing to remain obedient to God and His commands as they prepared to enter a land that would have some significant challenges. In the middle of his focus on God's undisputed faithfulness and constant presence with them, he turns their attention from God to themselves—specifically, their hearts and souls.

> "**Only take care, and keep your soul diligently**, lest you forget the things your eyes have seen, and lest they depart from your heart all the days of your life." (Deuteronomy 4:9 esv, emphasis added)

Moses knew that if they did not pay careful attention to their souls—and the things that shaped and defined their soul's true treasure and hope—they would forget what God had done and what He promised. The consequences of a soul not kept diligently would be so severe that generations after would be impacted by such negligence. Moses repeats this emphasis in Deuteronomy 6 when he says, "You shall love the LORD your God with all your **heart** and with all your **soul** and with all your **might**. And these words that I command you today shall be on your heart" (6:5–6, emphasis added).

It is not enough to go through the motions of keeping God's laws and commands, of practicing all the right practices but neglecting your soul. That's legalism. Jesus called out the Pharisees for that: "These people honor me with their lips, but their hearts are far from me" (Matthew 15:8; Isaiah 29:13). God takes no pleasure in our going through the motions. He wants our hearts, because our hearts both express and shape the condition of our souls.

Soul-care may not be our first instinct. Frequently, the first instinct is to either suck it up or give up. More than a few grandparents raising their grandchildren tell me they are just too tired and exhausted to carve out a quiet time, or to drag themselves to a support group, or to schedule another meeting with someone. They are consumed with having to deal with whatever urgent matter demands their attention.

You may feel the same. While there are no easy solutions or simple formulas for dealing with this problem, the truth is we are not made to function well in isolation. God made us relational creatures. We are made for relationship with other human beings and our Creator. He wants us to experience the blessing and strength of living in relationships where we actually practice the "one anothers" of the Bible—love one another, bear one another's burdens, exhort one another, encourage one another, build up one another (more on that in Chapter 8). God desires the very best for us, and He intends for us to grow and flourish in the context of community. Loneliness and feeling alone are among the most crippling states of the human soul and a leading cause of despair. That is not what God designed for us. We are sheep in a flock. It is one of the good things He gave to us for the sake of our souls.

Stand, Look, Ask, and Walk

God instructed Jeremiah to tell His people something they desperately needed to take to heart: "This is what the LORD says:

'**Stand** at the crossroads and **look; ask** for the ancient paths, ask where the good way is, and **walk** in it, and you will find rest for your souls'" (Jeremiah 6:16, emphasis added).

No human being escapes the consequences of choices made during the difficult times of their life. We encounter "crossroads" regularly, where we are faced with a crucial decision. What path will we choose? Sometimes the good way is obvious, but we don't take it because it's not the path we want or prefer. We think another path will be easier, but it never is.

Perhaps we just need a little dose of wisdom—or common sense. Or perhaps we simply need the encouragement of another to get us on the right path. I want to be that person to you.

When God spoke these words to Jeremiah, He knew the people would resist the path He calls "the good way." One of the reasons we do not take care of ourselves is because we believe we are fine. There may even be a bit of pride when we believe that we are "sacrificing" ourselves for the sake of our families.

Yet, when we assume this position, are we not rejecting the good way in favor of a futile way? Like the people in Jeremiah's day, we stubbornly declare, "We will not walk in it," because we think we know better.

If this is you, then I hope our journey through Psalm 23 has given you hope and an understanding of how much your Shepherd, the Lord Jesus Christ, desires for you to know and live in the sweet delight of His promised rest. It does require intentionality on your part—learning to come and wait.

Waiting is not passive. It is believing, trusting, hoping, and expecting God's answer in His actions. Waiting involves looking, asking, and walking where He leads. He simply asks you to submit to His guiding. He will take us to the place of rest and hope. As we practice this process of learning to wait and trust, here are two things I would challenge you to consider.

Prayer

"Prayer is simply conversing with God . . . opening our lives to God and acknowledging our total dependence on Him."[1] It is one of those disciplines for which we often find excuses to avoid. Why is prayer such a challenge for us? I think there are few of us who do not struggle with this discipline. While the reasons may vary for each of us, Deborah Haddix suggests seven ideas for helping us with this struggle.[2]

1. Give yourself permission to call out to God with an honest voice. The Psalms are a good place to go to realize God hears our prayers no matter how "messy" they may be.
2. Be specific in your honesty. Call out specifically anything you are worried about and ask for His help.
3. Train yourself to abide in prayer. This is the habit of resting in God's grace by asking Him to teach you how to pray, perhaps by praying Scripture.
4. Use your imagination. As you read the Word, imagine pictorial images, like a video in your mind.
5. Practice God's presence by simply sitting in His presence for several minutes before you start your day or as you go throughout the day.
6. Set your posture for prayer. There is no "correct" posture that must be followed, but your bodily posture before God is one way to help you engage your heart and mind.
7. Pray in conjunction with the practice of other disciplines, such as solitude and fasting.

Remember that spiritual disciplines become habits only when we choose to start practicing them. It doesn't happen by wishing it to be so. Prayer is one of those disciplines that we must choose to do because we believe it is important. It is a powerful path for soul rest.

Journaling

I know this discipline is hard for some, especially men. I know I struggle with it, but the more I do it, the more value I am reaping in my own walk with God. I don't do it every day, but I do journal several times a week. If it's hard for you, I understand, but I'm still not letting you off the hook. Your soul's health can be strengthened if you will choose to do it. Consider these few benefits of journaling.[3]

- Helps us build an authentic relationship with God
- Facilitates our learning about ourselves, our relationships, our life situations
- Provides clarity (brings out thoughts that might never have occurred otherwise)
- Helps make our thoughts and prayers more concrete
- Forces us to take time on a regular basis to sit with God and allow Him to shape our perspective on life through His eyes
- Marks out a time for us to listen as God speaks wisdom into our lives
- Facilitates connections to God, to ourselves, and to others as we ask probing questions, think through issues, and put the "stuff" tumbling around in our heads on paper
- Provides a safe place to observe and understand as we move toward change

Journaling can be an invaluable means of caring for your soul and increasing the effectiveness of other spiritual disciplines in your life. Journaling is something very personal but also very cathartic because it serves as both a connecting and cleansing process. It helps connect our hearts and souls to the Father's heart by conforming how we think to the mind of God. It helps to engage both our mind and heart in a process of putting things in perspective according to God's Word. In other words, we discover what is really true about a lot of things, including ourselves.

Remember that Jesus, who wants us to come and rest in Him, will take care of us. He is your Shepherd, and only He can give your soul what it needs. His care is not solely for our good but also for the sake of His name, that the trail of our life will clearly proclaim His goodness and mercy.

7

More Than Good Grandparents

When I think of life-altering moments in my life, there are two that particularly stand out: the arrival of our first child, and the day our first grandchild was born—the second generation of our flesh and blood. After all the excitement of the birth of our first child died down, I remember that I began to feel a sense of panic. I didn't know much about being a dad and all that would accompany my new role.

Diane and I found our lives ruled by diaper changing (before disposable diapers were a thing), sleepless nights, and trying to figure out the unintelligible communication attempts of our infant. We learned that discipline was necessary to adequately care for the needs of this new member of our family. It meant laying aside personal preferences for our social calendar and for a good night's sleep.

We also had to learn something about being courageous. As new parents, we often made decisions we believed were right for our child even when popular trends in child-rearing proclaimed something different. When our children were older, a new kind of courage was needed to trust them to make their own choices when we would have preferred to be the ones in control.

Grandparenting ushered another level of understanding and function. As grandparents, we were even more confused about this role. We had no idea what this grandparenting thing was supposed to look like and what our roles were supposed to be. For all we knew, grandparenting was summed up by the message on a T-shirt I had received:

GRANDPA'S TO-DO LIST

1. Spoil 'em.
2. Fill 'em up with sugar.
3. Send 'em home.

Beyond that, we had a lot of questions. Yes, our experience as parents taught us that we must pray for our grandchildren. We knew our lives ought to be an example of godly living for them. But was that all there was to it?

After founding and leading the Christian Grandparenting Network for more than two decades, one thing has become abundantly clear to us, both as parents and grandparents: Our children and grandchildren need the good news (the gospel of Christ) more than they need good gifts or good times. God's concern is not whether we are "good" grandparents; God's concern is how intentional we are about teaching our grandchildren to know, love, and follow Christ. I believe the primary role of every parent and grandparent is the same—tell the next generations the praiseworthy deeds of God (the gospel) and tell who He is and the wonders He has done. In other words, our greatest responsibility is to share the truth so that our grandchildren may know, love, and serve Christ with all their hearts.

I know that you, grandparents who are parenting your own grandchildren, also have questions about your role. You have your grandchildren 24/7. How do you juggle being both grand-parent and parent? Perhaps it's not so much about how your role differs from that of a typical grandparent, but to what degree that role is played out. And if there's one thing I've learned over the years about grandparenting (or parenting), it's this: It is all about intentionality.

Courageous grandparents are intentional grandparents. We are intentional in the way we provide for our grandchildren's basic needs—something that was hard enough as a young parent. We may try to teach them proper manners, respect, and politeness. They may learn from us how to ride a bike, drive a car, or practice the piano. Physical and emotional well-being matter, but never at the expense of that which matters for all eternity—their souls.

Courageous grandparents are intentional grandparents, especially when it comes to the gospel. Intentionality compelled by gospel faith requires both discipline and courage—discipline because it is tempting to look for the easy way, where minimal output is demanded, and courage because intentionality often means making hard decisions and swimming against the current of cultural norms. Gospel-shaped grandparents embody a conspicuous intentionality beyond simply being "good."

The gospel is the most important news and blessing that we could possibly offer our children and grandchildren. This is doubly true for you now, because you must serve as both parent and grandparent. The way the gospel shapes your life will have much to do with whether or not your grandchildren will want to embrace that same gospel transformation—or if they will want nothing to do with it.

In his book *Biblical Grandparenting*, Josh Mulvihill outlines eight practical ways the gospel ought to shape our lives as parents and grandparents.[1] I want to share three of those with you.

I believe these three marks ought to characterize our lives as grandparents (and parents) no matter our situation. However, I believe it is especially essential for those of you who are parenting your own grandchildren to grasp and put into practice.

Three Marks of Gospel-Shaped Grandparents

Jesus told us that those who abide in Him will bear much fruit. In fact, apart from Christ we cannot bear fruit (John 15:4–5). Gospel-shaped grandparents are abiders, which means they are fruit-bearers. Here are three key marks of fruit bearing (there are many more) as gospel-shaped grandparents:

Proclamation and Instruction

I must repeat something I alluded to earlier in this chapter, a statement often proclaimed by Josh Mulvihill in his writing and teaching: "Your grandchildren need the Good News more than they need good gifts from you."[2] Think about it.

Why would you be reluctant to share the most important thing about life and eternity with your grandchildren, yet willingly allow godless messages and perversions of the world to invade your home? You have no greater privilege than to share the good news with your grandchildren and teach them what is true. The gospel is the foundation upon which the entire building rests.

Instruction is that building. It is laying brick by brick the core truths of Scripture and then training our grandchildren to walk in that truth. We call it discipleship. In this age of relativism and secular humanism, our grandchildren need to know these truths. Ignorant of the truth, they will lack the ability to detect and deal with counterfeits.

Instruction also means we are prepared to help them learn to discern what is false from what is true when questions and doubts arise. In the Appendix I have included a few helpful resources that I hope you will find useful and effective.

Good instruction requires knowledgeable instructors. We cannot give what we do not have or teach what we do not know. Strive to be a student of the Word. You don't need a graduate degree to know and understand God's Word. After all, the Bible was given to those with little or no formal education. He sent the Spirit of truth to guide us in all truth. That's better than a PhD.

Our grandchildren will not be able to hold on to a faith that they do not understand and cannot defend. Neither will we. My grandson, Thomas, had doubts as a teenager, but the evidence was too strong for him to remain a doubter. You can guide your grandchildren to the evidence, where they can then know the truth and understand how to walk in it. It's what gospel-shaped grandparents do naturally and intentionally. Here are four practical ways you can do this in your home:

Make Family Time a Priority

I mentioned this earlier and it's worth highlighting again. The family table is one of the most sacred places in your home for developing trust and honest discussions where every member of the family is encouraged to participate. Do everything you can to protect this sacred space and make it a place where your grandchildren will always want to be participants. Read the Bible together, pray together, and process life over meals.

Bedtime is another one of the sacred spaces where you can read the Bible, talk about the events of the day, and process questions about life and faith. There also may be other family time opportunities that work for creating a safe place to talk about hard questions and to explore God's truth together. Family time is a time when each person values the other. That happens as we listen and create an environment that encourages open and honest conversations.

Family time is a time to unpack what the Bible says. It can be a time for a more structured Bible study, but it is mostly about learning and growing through participation and asking questions—not lecturing. There are few things more productive than reading the Bible together and talking about its relevance to life. Family Time Training has some great resources to help you with this.[3]

Make Christian Holidays Memorable

The Christmas and Easter seasons are prime opportunities to tell the story of God's salvation by grace. Open the Bible and read the stories of the incarnation (including OT references from Isaiah 7 and Micah 5) during Advent, and the crucifixion and the resurrection on Good Friday and Easter Sunday. Talk about why these events are so important to the gospel story. If you have younger children, invite them to help you act them out.

We are so bombarded with the world's messages about these uniquely Christian holidays that we can easily miss the real messages of hope and grace. Ask God to give you His Spirit of wisdom and understanding so you may guide your families toward knowing Him better and telling His story well.

Read Together Frequently

There is an abundance of good reading material available at the library, in bookstores, or online. Find books that tell God's story and stir the mind to imagine with wonder and awe that you can read with your grandchildren beginning at a very early age.

Lamplighter Publishing finds and reprints dozens of wonderful stories written more than one hundred years ago that tell the gospel story through the lives of children and adults in those periods.[4] Because the stories are written in and about a time in history that is so different from our own, they serve as great conversation starters with children.

Speak Blessing Often

I could spend a great deal of time talking about the importance of spoken blessing. Not only is it important for communicating to your grandchildren their value as someone created in the image of God, but it is a powerful tool for teaching a biblical worldview. This is one of the most powerful tools you can have in your family toolbox for communicating the gospel and putting it into practice.

We all know that words matter. We may pretend they don't, but they do. The words we speak communicate either cursing or blessing—death or life.

The Bible is clear that we who are alive in Christ ought "not let any unwholesome talk [cursing] come out of your mouths, but only what is helpful for building up others according to their needs, that it may benefit those who listen" (Ephesians 4:29). Paul understood the power of words, and we know the power your words will have in the life of a grandchild or a wayward adult child. How will you use the words you speak to benefit your household?

Here are two important things to understand about building a legacy of blessing and peace in your home:

(1) *Know the meaning and purpose of blessing.* To bless literally means to speak well of another; to praise. Speaking blessing is a declaration of that which is true. Your declaration of the truth that every human being is made in the image of

God and worthy of love carries enormous weight in the lives of grandchildren in your care.

They have likely already experienced more than their share of cursing. While they are in your care, you are a conduit through which God declares the truth about who they are and where their worth comes from. I'll say it again—make sure they know blessing is not limited to or based upon performance, so they do not mistakenly associate their worth with how well they perform. Simple statements can be transformational: "I love you so much." "Whenever I see you, you put a smile on my face." "I'm so glad you are part of our family."

When your grandchildren feel they failed at something that was important to them, turn it into a powerful time to speak a word of blessing to affirm their worth. For example, "Sammy, I'm so proud of how you handled that dropped ball today. I know that had to feel awful because it helped the other team win. But you were so courageous in the way you apologized to your teammates. Your character and integrity mean so much more to me than how well you play the game."

Consider the power of the words of blessing the Father spoke over His Son, Jesus: "This is my son, whom I love; with him I am well pleased" (Matthew 3:17). It might be easy for us to assume it was easy for the Father to say those words to Jesus. After all, He was the perfect Son.

That's true, yet I wonder if these words of blessing from the Father gave the human Jesus strength to endure, knowing what was coming. His humanity felt the weight of the price He would pay. That weight caused Him to ask the Father to take the cup away (Luke 22:42). Yet, the Father's blessing emboldened Him to place His trust in the Father and declare, "Yet, not what I will, but what you will" (Luke 22:42).

This blessing the Father declared over His Son illustrates two primary truths that ought to feature in any spoken blessing.

- **Value/Worth:** This is about identity—who your grandchildren are as image bearers of their Creator. The blessing proclaims value for who they are, not what they do, look like, or feel. When you speak blessing, you are declaring your firm conviction that God cherishes them uniquely . . . and so do you. Only human beings are made in His image, and in this truth is the reason they are valued so highly and loved so lavishly. The cross is the ultimate expression of that love.
- **Unique Purpose:** This is a declaration that says, "I believe in you and that God has a purpose for you as His child." Paul reminds us that we are "created in Christ Jesus to do good works, which God prepared in advance for us to do" (Ephesians 2:10). Blessing is a way to imagine with them what wondrous purposes God has in store.

(2) *Recognize the difference between prayers and blessing.* Simply stated, prayers are offered to God on behalf of others. Blessings are spoken over another on behalf of God. While similar, they are distinctly unique in form and objective. When you speak words of blessing, you are communicating not only your beliefs about them but also how God views them. You become the conduit through which God reveals himself and their own identity.

It's one thing to praise a child when they do something for which you are grateful and proud. That's good. It's another thing to proactively look for opportunities to express words of blessings that have nothing to do with something they did. Intentionality establishes a practice of speaking blessing regularly. Here are three simple ways to be intentional blessing givers:

- **Regular spoken blessings.** I like to use Numbers 6:24–26: "The LORD bless you and keep you; the LORD make his face shine on you and be gracious to you; the LORD turn his face toward you and give you peace." In my book *Courageous Grandparenting*, I go deeper into the significance of each of the phrases of the Numbers 6 blessing.[5] Such a blessing can have a profound impact on a child when it is spoken often. Bedtime, for example, is a great time to do this.

- **Milestone blessings.** Identify some of the specific milestones that will occur in your grandchild's life (birthdays, starting school, salvation, baptism, etc.). Write out and declare a special blessing for these moments. Your grandchildren will remember them, and it will make an impact.

- **Blessable moments.** Moses commanded the Israelites to impress critical truths upon the minds and hearts of their children. The same impression principle occurs when we look for opportunities to spontaneously speak words of blessing. Moses suggested four daily, natural moments in life for doing this (Deuteronomy 6:7):

  » When you sit at home (the family table)
  » When walk along the road (at the park, at the store, in the car)
  » When you lie down (bedtime)
  » When you rise (morning rituals)

Start the practice of speaking blessings in your home now. While the Scriptures do not command us to do this, there are plenty of examples of the power of blessing in the Bible and in the experiences of those who have taken it seriously enough to put into practice. Why would you not want to do this for the sake of those precious children God has entrusted to you? They desperately need to hear your genuine words of blessing.

To learn more about unleashing the power of spoken blessing, visit www.Christian Grandparenting.Net/Store and download a free *Creating a Legacy of Blessing* packet.[6]

Supplication

Supplication is a fancy way of referring to prayer. Gospel-shaped grandparents are praying grandparents. In the same way our salvation is not our own doing, our battles against the spiritual forces and powers of this dark world cannot be done in our own power. Only God's spiritual weapons can win those battles, through the power of the Holy Spirit. We are powerless to change hearts on our own. That is the work of God. Much prayer, much power. Little prayer, little power. There is no greater role of a grandparent than that of a prayer warrior.

I implore you to make it your regular practice not only to pray *for* your grandchildren in your care (and their parents) but also to pray *with* them. Be alert to those opportune moments to pray with them. Let prayer flow from those natural blessable moments we discussed earlier to speak of God's faithfulness and goodness. These are strategic ways to teach them to be thankful for His presence and goodness in Christ. Praying is a powerful way to teach and tell.

Check out the Appendix for a few prayer resources available to help you.

Imitation

Paul makes an audacious statement in his letter to the Philippians: "Whatever you have learned or received or heard from me, or seen in me—put it into practice" (4:9). It almost sounds like a dare, doesn't it? That is a pretty bold statement from a guy who once admitted that he was the "chief of sinners" (1 Timothy 1:15).

Paul declares that everyone transformed by the gospel ought to be able to say to those around them, and especially those of our own household, "Imitate me." This is not an arrogant assertion that we consider ourselves to be perfect. Paul already admitted he wasn't. No, Paul is proclaiming his confidence in God's grace. We can ask our grandchildren to imitate us precisely because we are imperfect and flawed.

You are saying to your grandchildren, "When I mess up—and I will—put into practice what I practice. Confession, admitting I'm wrong, and repentance, choosing to turn away from that sin and do what is right, will guide us in our mistakes." There are few words more powerful than "I am sorry. I was wrong. Will you forgive me?" Isn't that what you would delight to see imitated by your grandchildren?

Your grandchildren are with you 24/7. Let them know you welcome the opportunity to invite them to imitate what they hear you teach because what you teach is visible in your life—even when you mess up. Making sure our walk and our talk say the same thing is not a claim to perfection, but rather it is living under the grace and goodness of God, in which the most broken and flawed pieces of our lives are redeemed.

I believe the strongest and richest relationships happen when lives are shaped by the gospel. Gospel-shaped saints know a peace that surpasses understanding because they have a hope that is found only in the gospel, not in a futile attempt to measure up to some human standard. Sure, Jesus said we would have our share of trouble, but we "take heart" because He has overcome the world, and He promised to give us His peace—a peace that only God can give (John 16:33).

When my grandparents were alive, I remember a plaque that hung in their living room. It contained a poem by C. T. Studd.

> Only one life
> 'Twill soon be past;
> Only what's done
> For Christ will last.[7]

What about your legacy will last in the minds and hearts of those grandchildren you are raising right now? I would argue that it is not what is done *for* Christ but what is done *in* Christ that will last. Will they smell the aroma of Christ where the fragrances of grace, compassion, and humility abound? Or will the stench of anger, bitterness, and arrogance overpower? What about your life would you want them to imitate?

8

The One Another Factor

When Matt, one of my pastors, called me to ask if I could help someone named Rachel, I had no idea how much of a "*kairos moment*" it would be for me . . . and Rachel. Kairos moments are those moments in time when God unexpectedly sends an opportunity into your life that will drastically impact you and others in ways you could not have imagined. Some kairos moments can alter the trajectory of your life. While this one did not totally redirect my life trajectory, it certainly had a major impact on how that trajectory would play out for Rachel and me.

The only thing Matt told me about Rachel's story was that she and her husband had reached a tipping point. So, when I called her and asked to meet with them and another couple who had raised their own granddaughter, God's purpose behind this encounter was about to become clearer.

My awareness of the realities of raising grandchildren that day rose to a whole new level. It started me on a course of learning and engaging with others like you who would make the reason for this book so much more apparent. It also helped me realize how much those of us not living in your world are oblivious to your realities and how much more the body of Christ needs to know about those realities.

I am writing these next two chapters for two specific groups of people. This chapter is mainly for those who are raising grandchildren and struggling to feel like they belong to anything outside of their family. The next chapter is geared toward pastors and laity established in a local church who know there are grandparents parenting their own grandchildren in their community but have little or no personal involvement with them. In other words, this chapter is for those who feel invisible and the majority of us for whom those in the first group are essentially invisible.

Rachel and her husband, Lee, are part of the first group. After raising ten of their own children (all of them grown and nine doing well), they found themselves suddenly raising two of their grandchildren, born to their drug-addicted daughter, each by different fathers.

They were aware that they needed to be connected to others, but they did not know how to do that outside of their very small world. They also did not understand they might need to reach out to others as well. It's a common problem among grandparents in their situation. Rachel described it like this:

> I was tired and lonely but didn't trust many to be part of my inner circle, so I had no one to share my burdens with. I did not have the confidence necessary to open up to others without fear of being judged. Fear consumed me. The fear of having people know my story and my perceived failure disabled me. The shame I felt for my current situation tugged at my heart.

The thought of having to explain to a stranger how we got here was too much; I truly did not have the reserves. It simply just felt easier to be alone. I prayed God would send me a friend, but until then that hadn't happened.

Because of her husband's work schedule, Rachel often attended church alone. After dropping off the babies in the children's church, she would make her way to the worship center, trying to avoid eye contact with others. She would only briefly say hello to the pastor but never dared say anything more about their situation. She would then seek out a place where she could sit alone.

On one particular Sunday, however, Rachel realized the service was going to include a baby dedication ceremony.

I remember sitting in the pew as the tears rolled down my face. My heart was so broken thinking about my two adopted grandbabies who would never be up there on that stage where the church family would pray for them. Somehow, I'd convinced myself that we didn't belong up there. After all, we were just grandparents.

What would people say about us? Would they talk about us? Worse yet, would it just not seem normal? I told myself all the reasons why I didn't belong up there with all of these happy new parents. But something stirred inside of me that day.

After the service, I got up and headed toward the pastor. I caught his eye. My feet were walking, but my heart was running out of the church at full speed. I'm not sure how I got the courage up to go and speak to him, but there I was.

He greeted me warmly, and I introduced myself. Before the next sentence could get past my lips, I burst into tears and practically threw up on the poor man. It took more than a few attempts to share with him what I wanted to say. Truth is, I wasn't sure what I wanted to say. I felt God just urging me to tell him our story. Somewhere deep within me God gave me the courage to tell him all that I was feeling and about our need and desire to connect.

He sat with me and graciously listened as I managed to get out what I needed to say. I unfolded the story of my daughter's struggle with drugs and how she lost the babies to social services and how they had come to us. I explained that we didn't know where we fit in. We were too old to hang out with the young couples with their young children. And we were too young to fit in with the legacy group members who no longer had children living at home.

His compassion surprised me. His lack of awareness that there were families that were quietly sitting broken inside of his church validated my decision to not remain silent. This young pastor looked very perplexed, and then said the most wonderful thing: "I don't have a clue what to do with you, but I think I know someone who does!"

I was so relieved he hadn't asked us to leave or sent me to the elders, where I imagined being raked over the coals. He truly cared. He wanted to help. I was overwhelmed with gratitude and gave him a big hug.

We still laugh about that day. I'm so glad it is behind me, but I'm so proud that I did it. God met me there that day in that extremely awkward situation. He gave me the strength to step out, to show up, and to advocate for myself, my family, and other families like ours. I'm not going to lie, it was uncomfortable. Yet, surprisingly, I did not find the condemnation I expected, but instead was overwhelmed by love and compassion.

Perhaps you do not think you have the capacity to do what Rachel did—stand up and let your pastor know you need help too. Even when you manage to get to a weekend service, you may sit there overcome by the sense of crowded aloneness. No one knows your story, and if they did, you tell yourself they would avoid you like the plague. But are these feelings rooted in the truth, or is it something we have mistakenly allowed ourselves to believe?

We are all members of one body—the body of Christ. I think Rachel knew deep down there were probably those who would be willing to share her burdens if they knew about them. Still, it requires courage to step up and lay it all out there. "We can't predict how another may respond to our brokenness and our difficult stories," she says, "but I have learned not everyone needs to know and there are those for whom it will be too uncomfortable to step into our world. Yet, there are those precious few who will wrap their love and support around you. It is up to you to step out."

We are members of one another, and that includes you. Take heart from Paul's comments on this subject in both Romans and Ephesians. I urge you to read it again and ponder what it means.

> For by the grace given me I say to every one of you: Do not think of yourself more highly than you ought, but rather think of yourself with sober judgment, in accordance with the faith God has distributed to each of you. For just as each of us has one body with many members, and these members do not all have the same function, **so in Christ we, though many, form one body, and each member belongs to all the others.** We have different gifts, according to the grace given to each of us. (Romans 12:3–6, emphasis added)

> There is one body and one Spirit, just as you were called to one hope when you were called; one Lord, one faith, one baptism, one God and Father of all, who is over all and through all and in all. . . . So Christ himself gave the apostles, the prophets, the evangelists, the pastors and teachers, to equip his people

for works of service, so that the body of Christ may be built up until we all reach unity in the faith and in the knowledge of the Son of God and become mature, attaining to the whole measure of the fullness of Christ.

Then we will no longer be infants, tossed back and forth by the waves, and blown here and there by every wind of teaching and by the cunning and craftiness of people in their deceitful scheming. Instead, speaking the truth in love, we will grow to become in every respect the mature body of him who is the head, that is, Christ. From him the whole body, **joined and held together by every supporting ligament, grows and builds itself up in love, as each part does its work.** (Ephesians 4:4–5, 11–16, emphasis added)

As you read this, what struck you about who Paul says you are and what your purpose is? I hope you grasped the truth that if you have placed your faith and hope in the gospel of Jesus Christ, that gospel declares that you are His and you are made for His purposes. The sin debt we could not pay has been paid, and you are His forever. Now that you are His, He has made a way for you to live Life with a capital *L* to the praise of His glory.[1]

Because you are His child, you are also part of His body. We are all members of one another, not isolated units unrelated to one other. We are all joined together by "supporting ligaments"—the Spirit, His grace, and our connection with one another through Christ. It is those supporting ligaments that cause the entire body to grow and build itself up **as each part does its work.** We have been saved to live **as His body**, expressing itself through a variety of "one another" factors that characterize our relationship with one another to the glory and praise of our Father.

So, what does this mean practically, and why is it important? First, it is important because it is who we are in Christ. No one individual member can thrive and flourish apart from the other parts. We were not saved to be holy hermits. We were saved to live in unity as one body by one Spirit to encourage and build up one another. Our interpersonal relationships are critical for that to occur. It is inconceivable to think or say that I have no need for other members of the body. It is anathema to our Lord and a matter of great consequence for us.

Years ago, when I was new in my pastoral ministry role, I went through a very dark and painful time. My head was on the chopping block, and there was no shortage of people ready to swing the axe. However, two key people in that church stepped forward to tell me they believed in me and were prepared to walk with me through the fire if I was prepared to learn, grow, and not give up. They put into practice what a supporting ligament was about as they committed themselves to help me mature and grow in love. They did their part, and the result was that both the church and I were built up to the praise of God's glory.

They could have said, "It's not my problem. You figure it out." But they didn't. They believed it was a "body" matter, and they were committed to carrying out the commands to build up one another, exhort one another, and love one another.

In light of this glorious truth about being members of one another, I offer four practical ways to engage your faith community and bring your story that has been hidden into the light.

1. **Take seriously what the Bible says about the body of Christ.** In a world where the individual is supreme, we need to remember the truth about who we are and why we are here. We need one another because we are members of one another.

2. **Be bold without being brash.** It will take courage to go to your pastor like Rachel did. Do it for your sake and for the sake of the body. Share how you are feeling and that you know part of the reason you feel this way is because you have allowed yourself to believe a lie. However, be careful not to communicate that you expect the pastor to solve your problems. Offer to be part of the solution yourself. Ask for his or her counsel about ways to identify those in the congregation with similar stories and how best to engage them and the rest of the church family.

3. **Embrace the obstacles in your life as opportunities** for the body to do its part, and for God to reveal His glory and goodness. Your voice will allow others to help bear the burden. I only ask you to do so with the realization that we bear it together. We don't dump our burden on others to make them feel guilty. Rather, we explore together how to share it as members of one another.

4. **Pray for wisdom and understanding.** Pray for wisdom for yourself to know how to raise awareness among the leaders of your church about the growing number of grandparents in similar situations to yours. Pray for their understanding about this need and a willingness to seek God's wisdom for an appropriate response.

One final word from Rachel . . .

Joshua 1:9 tells us to "be strong and courageous. Do not be afraid; do not be discouraged, for the LORD your God will be with you wherever you go." Don't let Satan whisper lies in your ear. He will try to discourage you, tell you that you're not good enough, that you have made too many mistakes, and fill you with so much guilt that you give up and remain silent. But I tell you to stand firm in Christ, fight the good fight of faith. We are forgiven, we are made new in Christ, and we are loved by our heavenly Father.

Our stories may be hard and even ugly, but as I read through the Bible I am reminded that throughout human history, God's people have always lived hard stories and yet He has remained faithful. That has never changed.

9

A Plea to Pastors and Church Leaders

There is, perhaps, no group more critical to the solution of invisibility in the body of Christ for grandparents raising grandchildren than pastors and their staff. This isn't to put the onus on you as a pastor. It is simply to remind you that you are the key to reducing the invisibility and increasing the opportunities for the *ecclesia* of Christ in your care.[1] You are in a position to lead your flock into another opportunity where the body can demonstrate what it means to love one another as Christ loved us.

There is likely a significant and growing demographic in your congregation about which you may have little knowledge. While there have always been grandparents who are raising their grandchildren, never have we faced a growing epidemic like is occurring today. And never has this segment of the body of Christ been so invisible to us.

As long as pastors and elders remain uninformed about the growing numbers of families in this category, these grandparents and grandchildren will likely remain invisible to the rest of your congregation, and that will be a tragedy indeed. But my hope is not only to make you aware but also to encourage you to be a voice for these invisible members of Christ's body so that all parts of the body can work together and no one part be made to feel less important than another.

The federal government and many state agencies are awakening to this growing demographic in our society. Laws are being enacted to help provide resources because the financial, legal, and emotional cost is enormous. While I am grateful that our government is willing to provide assistance, I believe the church ought to be the first responders in this growing crisis in our country. It is the church that can provide real compassion and encouragement with no strings attached.

I am grateful that my home church has responded so passionately once it became aware of the need. We still have much work to do to find ways to minister to and with this amazing group of grandparents. There are still more ways to raise awareness in our church and all the churches in our community, but the journey has begun.

Perhaps you are already leading your faith community in addressing this need. If so, I applaud you. On the other hand, maybe this is the first you have heard of this need area. Perhaps in your community it is not a need, at least not yet. Whatever the situation or state of progress in your church, I urge you to consider the following ways you can make sure that each is doing their part so that the whole body is being built up in love and thus attaining to the full measure of Christ.

Bring the need to your elders or deacons. Invite one or more couples who are raising their grandchildren to share their stories. Proactively look for grandparents in your congregation who are in this situation. Invite members of the congregation and staff to hear their stories. Find those who would be willing to learn how to ask the right questions about what these grandparents need and be willing to pray for them and share with them opportunities and resources the church provides to help them.

Finally, include grandparents who are raising their grandchildren in your strategies for family ministry. Here are a few simple ways to do that without creating another major ministry program.

1. **Parenting events.** Include grandparents in parenting events you plan at the church. When you have classes on parenting or discipleship, make sure grandparents who are raising their grandchildren are also included.

2. **Baby dedications.** Invite them to stand with other parents of young children and dedicate their grandchildren whom they are now parenting.

3. **Respite days.** In our church, we often offer scheduled respite days when parents can drop off their children and have a day to do something on their own. The church provides qualified childcare and activities for the kids during the allotted time (usually 9–4) on designated days, twice per year. This is particularly targeted for single moms, but why not invite grandparents who are raising their grandkids to participate?

4. **Congregational orientation.** Offer a potluck or dessert time following a weekend service for the whole congregation to learn more about this part of our church family. Invite two or three grandparents to share their stories and recognize all those in attendance who have similar stories. Use this as a time to discuss ways the church family can come alongside these grandparents.

5. **Surrogate grandparents.** Enlist surrogate grandparents, people who serve as the "grandparents" for a family, to do what the biological grandparents are not able to do because they must be the "parents" now.

6. **Resource center.** Set up a place where any church could refer grandparents for legal, financial, childcare, and emotional counseling resources. Partner with other churches in the area for grandparents in similar situations, and ask people to pray about helping set up such a resource center.

7. **Mentorship.** Pair parents with grandparents raising children of a similar age to pray with each other and help each other navigate some of the challenges of registering in school, purchasing school supplies, and other parenting concerns.

8. **Preach and teach.** When you preach on parenting, include and affirm grandparents, too, especially those raising their grandchildren. Don't assume that because you say "parent" they understand you are talking to them. If you don't know that grandparents are addressed as much as parents in Scripture, I urge you to familiarize yourself with current resources on grandparenting.[2]

Pastor, God has called you to lead a local part of the ecclesia of Christ by teaching, preaching, and shepherding those under your care. I believe one of the key and essential roles of a pastor is to see that every family is adequately equipped to disciple the next generations so they will know, love, and serve Christ. Grandparents are part of that family—*all* grandparents, not only grandparents raising their grandchildren. As such, they also must be included in the training and equipping processes under your leadership.

I hope you will not interpret what I am proposing to you as the creation of another separate ministry in your already full programming strategy. Rather, see this as an opportunity to reassess and strengthen your family ministry philosophy. The question is, how do we do family ministry in such a way that we do not leave out any one part of the family? Will we build a family ministry model that is culturally driven or biblically driven? A biblically driven model is one in which every member of the body of Christ is valued and engaged.

Grandparents raising grandchildren are an essential part of the family God calls us to equip through effective discipleship for the sake of another generation. We do not want to see Judges 2:10 reoccur in our time: "Another generation grew up who knew neither the LORD nor what he had done for Israel." Help us fight for all our families, regardless of their circumstances.

APPENDIX

Finding Help for Your Specific Situation

Finally Home Family Strengthening Events

WWW.FINALLYHOME.NET

The mission of Finally Home is to strengthen foster, kinship, and adoptive families. Finally Home understands that raising grandchildren is a form of adoption and addresses the church's role in supporting the families of grandparents who are parenting their grandchildren.

Christian Grandparenting Network

WWW.CHRISTIANGRANDPARENTING.NET

Christian Grandparenting Network is dedicated to helping equip grandparents in every situation to fulfill their God-given roles. They offer resources and services that support grandparents who are parenting their grandchildren full-time and connect these families with groups like the Grand Family Coalition (www.grandfamily coalition.org). The Grand Family Coalition is dedicated to serving grandparents and other kin raising kin by providing assistance in connecting with federal services and helping families find local services in their area.

Prayer Resources

Stormie Omartian, *The Power of a Praying Grandparent* (Eugene, OR: Harvest House Publishers, 2016).

Lillian Penner, *Grandparenting with a Purpose: Effective Ways to Pray for Your Grandchildren* (Enumclaw, WA: Redemption Press, 2015). www.grandparentingwithapurpose.com

Sherry Schumann, *Prayers That Stir the Hearts of Grandparents* (self-pub., 2019). www.sherryschumann.com

Family Time Resources

Tina Houser, *Heirlooms: Passing Faith Stories to Your Grandchildren* (Anderson, IN: Warner Press, 2019).

Marty Machowski, *Long Story Short: Ten-Minute Devotions to Draw Your Family to God* (Greensboro, NC: New Growth Press, 2010).

Family Time Training (www.famtime.com) offers numerous resources for parents/grandparents to build effective family discipleship in the home.

Roots Kids Worship (www.gospelshapedfamily.com) is music sung by kids for kids that forms and fortifies faith. Children learn God's Word as they sing key Bible verses and doctrine put to many genres of music. Perfect for the car, classroom, or living room.

Reading Resources

Recommended Grandparenting Books

Cavin Harper, *Courageous Grandparenting: Building a Legacy Worth Outliving You* (Colorado Springs: ElderQuest Ministries, 2019).

Josh Mulvihill, *Biblical Grandparenting: Exploring God's Design for Disciple-Making and Passing Faith to Future Generations* (Minneapolis: Bethany House Publishers, 2018).

Josh Mulvihill, ed., *Equipping Grandparents: Helping Your Church Reach and Disciple the Next Generation* (Minneapolis: Bethany House Publishers, 2018).

Larry E. McCall, *Grandparenting with Grace: Living the Gospel with the Next Generation* (Greensboro, NC: New Growth, 2019).

Miscellaneous Recommended Reading

Josh Mulvihill, *Biblical Worldview: What It Is, Why It Matters, and How to Shape the Worldview of the Next Generation* (Roanoke, VA: Renewanation, 2019).

Josh Mulvihill, *Preparing Children for Marriage* (Phillipsburg, NJ: P&R Publishing, 2017).

Martha Evans Sparks, *Raising Your Children's Children* (Kansas City, MO: Beacon Hill, 2011).

Elaine K. Williams, *The Sacred Work of Grandparents Raising Grandchildren* (Bloomington, IN: Balboa, 2011).

NOTES

Introduction

1. Generations United, "Raising the Children of the Opioid Epidemic: Solutions and Support for Grandfamilies," 2018, www.gu.org/app/uploads /2018/09/Grandfamilies-Report-SOGF-Updated.pdf, 1.

2. Generations United, 2.

Chapter 2: The Guilt-Blame Trap

1. Martha Evans Sparks, *Raising Your Children's Children: Help for Grandparents Raising Grandkids* (Kansas City: Beacon Hill, 2011), 103.

2. Abraham Piper, "Let Them Come Home," *Decision*, August 28, 2007.

Chapter 4: You Keep Using That Word

1. "Grandparents Finally Get the Spotlight They Deserve," *Medill News Service*, August 30, 2018, https://dc.medill.northwestern.edu/blog/2018/08/30/ grandparents-finally-get-spotlight-deserve/#sthash.GKDRTOdj.dpbs.

Chapter 5: You Can't Give What You Do Not Have

1. Joanna Mikhail, "What Is Biblical Self-Care and How Can I Practice It?" *Blog.Bible*, October 1, 2017, https://blog.bible/bible-engagers-blog/entr /what-is-biblical-self-care-and-how-can-i-practice-it.

2. Phillip Keller, *A Shepherd Looks at Psalm 23* (Grand Rapids, MI: Zondervan, 1970), 16.

Chapter 6: Shepherd-Driven Soul Care

1. Deborah Haddix, *Soul Nourishment: Satisfying Our Deep Longing for God* (Anderson, IN: Warner, 2018), 39.

2. Haddix, 39–40.

3. Haddix, 244–245.

Chapter 7: More Than Good Grandparents

1. Josh Mulvihill, *Biblical Grandparenting* (Minneapolis: Bethany House Publishers, 2018), 155–171.

2. Josh Mulvihill, *Grandparenting* (Minneapolis: Bethany House Publishers, 2018), 116.

3. For more resources, visit the Family Time Training website at www.famtime.com.

4. Lamplighter Books provides character-building stories from all times, built on the foundation of God's Word. For more information, visit their website at https://lamplighter.net/c/.

5. Cavin Harper, *Courageous Grandparenting: Building a Legacy Worth Outliving You* (Colorado Springs: ElderQuest Publishing, 2018), 107.

6. Christian Grandparenting Network is committed to empowering and equipping grandparents to live with biblical intentionality so that another generation will know, love, and serve Christ. CGN offers conferences/seminars, books, blogs, GrandCamps, and other resources to help grandparents fulfill their biblical roles.

7. From the poem "Only One Life" by C. T. Studd, missionary and founder with Heart of Africa Mission (now WEC) in China, India, and the African Congo.

Chapter 8: The One Another Factor

1. Life with a capital *L* refers to spiritual life that is the result of the transformational power of the gospel by grace through faith (Ephesians 2), and that the glory of God is an individual who is fully alive. See Matt Heard's *Life with a Capital L: Embracing Your God-Given Humanity* (Colorado Springs: Multnomah, 2014).

Chapter 9: A Plea to Pastors and Church Leaders

1. *Ecclesia* is the word the New Testament uses that is most often translated as *church*, though the word *church* is not the best representation of this Greek word. The Greek word *kuriakon* might better be translated *church*. While there are many nuances of the meaning of *ecclesia* that are not represented by *church*, I will simply say that whereas *church* tends to suggest a place or building, *ecclesia* suggests an assembly of people.

2. The Appendix lists several grandparenting resources I would recommend to any pastor who wants to build an effective ministry to and with grandparents. All of these are available on the Legacy Coalition website (www.thelegacycoalition.com).

ACKNOWLEDGMENTS

This is a writing project I would likely have abandoned long ago had it not been for Rachel Mahnke. She, more than anyone else I know, gave me a reason to write this book. I owe a huge debt of thanks to Rachel for energizing me to finish the project. Rachel and Lee's story has opened my eyes to so many other stories of men and women who have grieved over the choices of their adult children, and the impact those choices have had on the grandchildren and their own expectations as grandparents.

Rachel's passion and determination motivated me to write about grandparents who raise their grandchildren. She inspired me to write it so those of us who live outside of the realities of grandparents like Rachel and Lee can understand how we fit into their stories. How do we encourage and support these grand-families and make them feel welcome in God's family, where they belong?

Thank you, Rachel, for your passion, your courage, and your constant encouragement to tell the stories that we all need to hear. Thank you for your contribution to this book and your belief that the church must offer hope to families like yours.

Thank you for the constant reminder that as challenging as your role is as a grandparent parenting your grandchildren, it is also an amazing opportunity to impact these little ones God has entrusted to you.

My thanks also go out to two people from my home church, Woodmen Valley Church in Colorado Springs—Matt Ferrell, campus pastor, and Cheryl Howard, senior director of Woodmen Kids. Matt dramatically pulled me into this grand-family arena through a divinely appointed phone call. Since that time, he has continually participated with Rachel and me to find ways to engage the church. Cheryl's constant enthusiasm and support of this work has kept me from giving up on this project. Thank you, Matt and Cheryl, for not giving up on me.

Cavin Harper

Soli Deo Gloria

Cavin Harper is the founder and former president of the Christian Grandparenting Network, and the author of *Courageous Grandparenting*, *A DIY GrandCamp Field Guide*, and *Wayfinder*. He has also been a contributing author for the Legacy Coalition and Joni and Friends, as well as hosting a radio talk show called *Not on Our Watch* and the *Family Impact* podcast. He travels as a speaker and presenter of his Courageous Grandparenting seminars and is a featured speaker for Gospel Shaped Family Conferences and select conference events throughout the United States and Canada. Cavin and his wife, Diane, also created GrandCamps, a three- to five-day faith adventure for grandparents and grandchildren. Cavin and Diane were married in 1969 and have two daughters and nine grandchildren. They make their home in Colorado Springs, Colorado. You can find Cavin's weekly blog, *Courageous Grandparenting*, at GospelShapedFamily.com.

Josh Mulvihill is the executive director of church and family ministry at Renewanation. He has served as a pastor for nearly twenty years, serves on the board of AWANA, provides leadership to the Christian Grandparenting Network, and has a PhD from the Southern Baptist Theological Seminary. Josh is the author or editor of nine books including *Biblical Grandparenting*, *Preparing Children for Marriage*, and *Biblical Worldview*. Josh's primary ministry, and greatest joy, is being a husband and father. He is married to Jen, and they have five children. Josh blogs at GospelShapedFamily.com.